Designing Adaptive and Personalized Learning Environments

Designing Adaptive and Personalized Learning Environments provides a theoretically based yet practical guide to systematic design processes for learning environments that facilitate automatic customization of learning and instruction.

The book consists of four main parts: In "Introduction and Overview," the concepts of adaptivity and personalization are introduced and explored in detail. In "Theoretical Perspectives with Example Applications," various theoretical concepts underlying adaptive and personalized learning are discussed, including cognitive profiling, content-based adaptivity, exploration-based adaptivity, and mobile and ubiquitous settings. In "Practical Perspectives with Example Applications," the implementation process for adaptive and personalized learning environments is described, followed by application in various contexts. In "Validation and Future Trends," various evaluation techniques for validating the efficiency and efficacy of adaptive and personalized learning systems are discussed. This final part concludes with a discussion of emerging trends in adaptive and personalized learning research.

Based on cutting-edge research, *Designing Adaptive and Personalized Learning Environments* is appropriate as a primary textbook for both undergraduate and graduate courses focused on the design of learning systems, and as a secondary textbook for a variety of courses in programs such as educational technology, instructional design, learning sciences, digital literacy, computer-based systems, and STEM content fields.

Kinshuk is Associate Dean of Faculty of Science and Technology and Full Professor in the School of Computing and Information Systems at Athabasca University, Canada. He also holds the NSERC/CNRL/Xerox/McGraw Hill Industrial Research Chair for Adaptivity and Personalization in Informatics. He is founding chair of IEEE Technical Committee on Learning Technologies, and founding editor of the *Journal of Educational Technology and Society* and the *Smart Learning Environments* journal.

Interdisciplinary Approaches to Educational Technology

Series Editor: J. Michael Spector

Current and forthcoming series titles:

Foundations of Educational Technology: Integrative Approaches and Interdisciplinary Perspectives
  J. Michael Spector

Design for Learning in Virtual Worlds
  Brian C. Nelson and Benjamin E. Erlandson

Foundations of Educational Technology: Integrative Approaches and Interdisciplinary Perspectives, Second Edition
  J. Michael Spector

Educational Technology Program and Project Evaluation
  J. Michael Spector and Allan H.K. Yuen

Designing Adaptive and Personalized Learning Environments
  Kinshuk

Designing Adaptive and Personalized Learning Environments

KINSHUK

Routledge
Taylor & Francis Group

NEW YORK AND LONDON

First published 2016
by Routledge
711 Third Avenue, New York, NY 10017

and by Routledge
2 Park Square, Milton Park, Abingdon, Oxon OX14 4RN

Routledge is an imprint of the Taylor & Francis Group, an informa business

Library of Congress Cataloging in Publication Data
Names: Kinshuk, 1970– author.
Title: Designing adaptive and personalized learning environments / Kinshuk.
Description: New York, NY : Routledge, 2016. | Series: Interdisciplinary
    approaches to educational technology | Includes bibliographical references
    and index.
Identifiers: LCCN 2015041684| ISBN 9781138013056 (hardback) | ISBN
    9781138013063 (pbk.) | ISBN 9781315795492 (ebook)
Subjects: LCSH: Individualized instruction. | Computer-assisted instruction.
    | Web-based instruction. | Instructional systems—Design. | Learning,
    Psychology of.
Classification: LCC LB1031 .K4145 2016 | DDC 371.39/4—dc24
LC record available at http://lccn.loc.gov/2015041684

ISBN: 978-1-138-01305-6 (hbk)
ISBN: 978-1-138-01306-3 (pbk)
ISBN: 978-1-315-79549-2 (ebk)

Typeset in Minion Pro, Helvetica Neue and Copperplate Gothic
by Florence Production Ltd, Stoodleigh, Devon, UK

Printed and bound in the United States of America by Publishers Graphics,
LLC on sustainably sourced paper.

Contents

Acknowledgments   vii

PART I
INTRODUCTION AND OVERVIEW   1

CHAPTER 1—Defining Adaptivity and Personalization   3

CHAPTER 2—Adaptivity and Personalization in Life-Long Learning   19

CHAPTER 3—Contexts   29

PART II
THEORETICAL PERSPECTIVES WITH EXAMPLE
APPLICATIONS   41

CHAPTER 4—Cognitive Profiling   43

CHAPTER 5—Content-Based Adaptivity and Personalization   59

CHAPTER 6—Adaptivity and Personalization in Exploration-Based
Learning   77

CHAPTER 7—Adaptivity and Personalization in Mobile and
Ubiquitous Settings   93

PART III
PRACTICAL PERSPECTIVES WITH EXAMPLE APPLICATIONS   109

CHAPTER 8—Implementation Process of Adaptive and Personalized
Learning Environments   111

CHAPTER 9—Adaptivity and Personalization of Learning in Various
Contexts   125

CHAPTER 10—Reusability in Adaptive and Personalization Learning   139

PART IV
VALIDATION AND FUTURE TRENDS   151

CHAPTER 11—Evaluation of Adaptive and Personalized Systems   153

CHAPTER 12—Future Development and Research Issues   165

Index   177

Acknowledgments

I wish to thank my wife Dorota Mularczyk and children Gauri Maria and Sahaj Gabriel for their love, support, and, most of all, patience as I spent hours and hours over many months creating and recreating several iterations of each chapter. I also thank Mike Spector, series editor, and Alex Masulis, senior editor at Routledge, for their encouragement, patience, and guidance throughout the process. Last but not least, my thanks go to Daniel Schwartz for making the final editing and production a breeze.

part one
INTRODUCTION
AND OVERVIEW

one
Defining Adaptivity and Personalization

Online learning has come a long way since its emergence in mainstream education in the mid-90s. Significant growth in both hardware and software technologies in recent years have now made it a real possibility to remove barriers to education and widen the access for those who are not able to come to a physical campus. However, the majority of current implementations of learning environments lack the support individual students need to achieve success in their learning. This is not to say that there are no possibilities to support each and every student individually in achieving success in their learning. There is a whole range of tools, techniques and pedagogies that can facilitate such individual support in online learning. This book is designed to provide both conceptual understanding and practical solutions to systematically design learning environments that provide automatic customization of learning and instruction to individual learners.

Many of us would be able to recall experiences from our past, when we struggled in the classroom because the teacher's explanations were not making sense, or we got bored because what was being taught we already knew. But it was impossible to ask the teacher to do something differently because the teacher needed to take care of the whole class and not just one student. Fast forward to today, almost every educational institution has now embraced some form of online learning, whether as a supplement to their traditional face-to-face teaching or to provide certain courses specifically in an online mode. The situation, however, has not changed.

Various types of learning environments have emerged to support different learning activities. Most popular types are content management systems (CMS), learning management systems (LMS) and social platforms. Most of these environments are primarily teacher-driven, providing various tools and functionality to support various teaching tasks. For example, teachers can create several learning units in LMS, provide various quizzes to learners, structure the whole learning sequence, and make discussion forums available to students. All students in one course then see and experience exactly the same content, navigation, presentation and other aspects of the course, despite the fact that they may be from different backgrounds, may have different preferences for learning activities, have different media preferences, already know some of the content, and have achieved different competence levels in various topics of that course. These environments, by their nature, are designed to run multiple courses at a time, involving a large number of students, and are not expected to provide a customized learning experience to individual students.

Environments with adaptivity and personalization focus on the process of learning differently. They focus on individual differences of students, and based on certain criteria, customize learning to suit individual students. Learning process in such environments does not require each and every student to follow a pre-determined rigid path. Instead, content, activities, navigation, presentation, interaction and other aspects of the course are adapted and personalized to the real-time context of the individual student.

Let us look at the two terms we have been using: adaptivity and personalization. What do they mean and how are they related to each other?

Adaptivity

When a teacher is teaching a class, adaptivity means continuously looking at the impact of teaching approaches on the students, and changing various aspects of teaching to improve student learning. In an online environment, this enables learning environments to analyze the learning processes of individual students on a continuous basis, and allows them to make modifications geared towards better learning outcomes. For example, the environment can recommend to every student who did not show sufficient competency in a quiz, to go through the associated learning unit again before proceeding to the next unit.

Personalization

Let us take an example of two students learning a particular accounting concept in an online environment. One student comes from a family running a small business. Another student comes from a family of farmers. Personalization of learning for both students would mean understanding their backgrounds and providing them with practice cases that they can relate to. For the student with the business background, a case from a factory scenario would provide a more familiar situation to relate to, whereas for the student with the farming background, a case based on a farming situation would provide better familiarity.

Dimensions of adaptivity and personalization

Adaptivity and personalization are, in some sense, two sides of the same coin. Adaptivity can be seen as a perspective from the learning environment's side, whereas personalization considers an individual student's perspective. Both ultimately aim to improve learning for individual students by increasing student's efficiency, effectiveness, and satisfaction. These three aspects are not always in sync with each other. For example, increase in efficiency may require focusing only on important concepts, but that approach may affect effectiveness of the learning process and even lead to reduced satisfaction.

Compared with other scenarios, learning situations also have their unique characteristics when it comes to student efficiency, effectiveness and satisfaction. For example, in an office environment, efficiency is increased by reducing the amount of duplication. However, in learning, revision of content and practice of associated skills are important for achieving mastery.

It is important to note that the better a learning environment is able to understand the student and their learning goals, the better it will be able to provide adaptivity and personalization. At the same time, the more the student understands the capabilities and limitations of the learning environment, the more realistic his/her expectations would be towards what to expect from the learning environment. In other words, the better the student and the learning environment will understand each other, the better adaptivity and personalization will take place.

The concept of adaptivity and personalization has been around for a long time both within learning domains, and in other areas. For example, Michael Hannafin and Kyle Peck discussed characteristics of a good (effective) computer aided-instruction environment in as early as the 1980s (Hannafin & Peck, 1988). Oppermann (1994) categorized adaptive environments ranging from system initiated adaptivity with no user control, to user initiated adaptability where the environment provides various tools to the user for customizing system behaviour but does not change behaviour itself. In between these two extremes are the stages of system initiated adaptivity with pre-information to the use about the changes, user selection of adaptation from system suggested features, and user desired adaptability supported by tools and performed by the system (Oppermann, Rashev & Kinshuk, 1997).

Test your understanding

1. Which of the following would be example(s) of adaptivity and/or personalization?

    a. A teacher gives an assignment to all students in a class after three lecture classes.
    b. A teacher tells a student to study section four of chapter three again after the student received low marks in the assignment.
    c. A student searches on the Internet for suitable content after getting low marks in a test.
    d. A student retakes a course after failing it the first time.

2. Which of the following factor(s) would be suitable for consideration to provide adaptivity and/or personalization?

a. student's name
b. student's age
c. student's driver's license number
d. student's preference for videos

Need for adaptivity and personalization

In online learning environments, it is possible for students to learn at their own pace, without the restriction of time and location. While this flexibility provides convenience to students and is seen as a positive feature, it can also create situations where students may find themselves without the presence of a teacher at the time they are learning. The online nature of learning environments also enables students from anywhere in the world to learn from the same environment. This leads to time zone differences, once again creating the possibility that an expert may not be available when students need help. Adaptivity and personalization in these scenarios aim to fill the gap created due to the absence of the teacher by providing appropriate support, help and feedback to the students. Adaptivity and personalization methods also help with customizing environment behaviour so that the students do not have to spend time learning how to use the environment instead of focusing on actual learning tasks.

How does adaptivity work?

The principle ingredient of adaptivity and personalization is that the learning environments monitor what each individual student is doing. They look for any action patterns—any sequence of actions, that can lead to problems students may face. By monitoring these action patterns, through different components of environment's interface where the student is interacting with the environments, these environments try to find if there are ways in which, first of all, students' errors could be corrected, and second, how students' learning process through the environment could be improved and made more efficient. Some environments also support students in the learning phase by introducing them to various system operations. Learning environments are complex by nature. Complex environments typically have lots of different functions, and it is not easy for the users of such environments to know all the different functionalities that are available. Let us take an example of a word processing application. Not everyone is familiar with managing "reference sources" or with inserting "table of authorities". In other words, there are so many functions in these applications that many of us may not use, even after using these applications for years. In the context of learning environments, if there was a way to find out what students really need and whether they are currently using the system functionality appropriately, the environments could provide certain help or support to the students to make them familiar with those functions. That would make students' learning process much more efficient.

Some environments draw students' attention to unfamiliar tools. If a student is doing an activity in a certain environment, and the adaptivity and personalization mechanism finds that there is a better way to do it because there is a readily available function or tool in the environment to do that task more efficiently, then the environment can introduce that function or tool to the student.

The main driver for adaptivity and personalization mechanism in the learning environments is the situations when students make errors during the learning process. When a student is using the learning environment appropriately, then the adaptivity and personalization mechanism remains inert. However, it keeps monitoring student's actions. As and when the student makes a mistake in the learning process, such as selecting a wrong parameter in a simulation or incorrectly answering a quiz, the mechanism then kicks in and checks why the student made that mistake. A good adaptivity and personalization mechanism does not just inform the student that he/she has made a mistake; instead, it tries to identify why the mistake was made and what was the cause of it. It then tries to remedy that cause by recommending certain remedial content to the student, or by changing the system behaviour, such as providing content in the format more suitable for that particular student.

Benefits of adaptivity and personalization

In a typical classroom, there are lots of students and it is impossible for teachers to provide proper support to each and every student's needs. Some students in the class would typically succeed even without the teacher. These students are well-versed in the learning process and they are typically in the top range of the class. Then there are other students who are in the bottom range and are probably not prepared for that particular course. However, there remains a large range of students in the middle who would do much better with some support, but that support needs to be customized. Students have different backgrounds, they have different preferences, and they learn differently. Individual students have different approaches regarding how they understand the material and how they can get the skills in a more effective and efficient way. Therefore, in a typical classroom with a large number of students, it is not possible for one teacher to provide all that support. That is where adaptivity and personalization comes in. The adaptivity and personalization mechanism looks at individual student's needs, their characteristics, backgrounds, competencies, mental abilities, behavioural preferences, effective states, and so on. Based on these parameters, the adaptivity and personalization mechanism can recommend what kind of learning experience would best suit each individual student.

For example, if there is a student with a particular level of cognitive abilities, let us say, a student who has a low working memory capacity. Such a student will not be able to keep too much information at a time in his/her mind for immediate processing. On the other hand, there is another student who has a higher working memory capacity and therefore can do a lot of calculations in their mind. These students need to be taught differently. Depending on the aim of the learning process, adaptivity and personalization may help the first student who has a low working memory capacity, by providing material that does not require a lot of immediate calculations. On the other hand, the teacher may decide 'No, this student needs to learn how to compensate for his/her low working memory capacity.' In that case, the adaptivity and personalization mechanism may challenge that student by providing the content that requires intermediate calculations that the student has to do in his/her mind. Another example could be based on learning styles. Students have different learning styles; some students like to first get an overview of the whole material before going into detail, whereas other students like to go through the material sequentially rather than getting overwhelmed by the overview of the content. So different students have different needs because of their different characteristics, and adaptivity and personalization can provide benefit to all these different students by monitoring the needs of the individual students.

Student characteristics

Different characteristics of the students can be used in various aspects of adaptivity and personalization. For example, they can help in providing adaptive navigation guidance in the learning environment, selecting the level of granularity of the domain content to provide to the student at a certain point in time, identifying whether the student will learn effectively from analogies or not, and so on.

These student characteristics can be classified as follows:

- Behavioral attributes: These include various characteristics related to the students' personal behaviors, such as preferences of the student, familiarity with the exploration process, and familiarity with various types of multimedia objects. Behavioral attributes can be solicited through direct inputs from the students, such as through questionnaires.
- Performance attributes: These attributes are related to the students' competency in the subject matter, such as the level of the student's current understanding of the domain content, his/her experiences within the domain, and competency in domain related skills. Performance attributes can be identified through quizzes, tests and other similar assessment mechanisms.
- Cognitive attributes: These attributes are related to the student's cognitive load capacity. They require understanding of the student's cognitive abilities. Examples include working memory capacity that allows humans to keep a limited amount of information active for a short period of time, inductive reasoning ability that enables construction of concepts from examples, information processing speed that determines how fast the students can acquire information correctly, and associative learning skill that enables linking of new knowledge to existing knowledge.
- Physiological attributes: These attributes are related to the student's physical state. They can be analyzed by measuring various physical parameters. For example, students' stress levels can be calculated by checking the heart rate variability. Similarly, the skin temperature, pupil dilation, rate of perspiration and other such parameters can help in understanding the student's current physical state.

Limitations and problems of adaptivity and personalization

While adaptation has lots of benefits for students, there are also certain problems and limitations that need to be understood. First of all, to provide any adaptation and personalization, the environment has to monitor what the student is doing, what the student's characteristics are, what are the student's preferences, and various other information about the student. This means that the student will be observed by the environment. The student's actions will be recorded, and therefore data and privacy protection issues need to be considered. Who has access to that data? What can that person or organization do with that data? Can the data be misused? Also, if that information can be accessed by different people, then social monitoring becomes a possibility. For example, if a student did not succeed in a particular quiz in their first attempt and that information gets in the hands of other students or a potential employer, then that can have significant implications. Environments with adaptivity and personalization provide recommendations to the students regarding certain types of content, certain types of navigation, and other aspects of the learning experience. The students may therefore feel that they are being manipulated by the environment. Such recommendations are made by the environment based on the monitoring of the student, and the inferences made by the environment on the data collected during monitoring. If the environment's inferences about the student are wrong, then the student may not get what he/she should actually be getting. That may frustrate the student and may also hinder the learning process.

Another issue to consider is that adaptive and personalized learning environments, like all other online systems, are designed by human system designers and programmed by computer programmers. Whatever functionality is provided in the environment is what designers thought the students would need. In other words, the learning environments are really a representation of designers' perspective of students' needs. Students are therefore exposed to the adaptation concept favoured by the designer of the environment. If the designer thinks that the students need a particular type of adaptation, then that is what the students will have. Otherwise the students will not have that particular adaptation even if they wanted that type of adaptation.

Another problem with adaptivity and personalization is that they change the learning environment's behaviour. For example, when a student is using a learning environment, initially the environment may be providing content in a certain way, but after inferring that the student has a certain preference, the adapativity and personalization mechanism will change the system's behaviour to accommodate for that student preference. The consequence of that is the interface representation and the content will now be presented in a different way than before. This may come as a surprise to the student if he/she is not expecting such a change. The student may get distracted from the learning task that he/she is currently doing by sudden automatic modifications that happen due to adaptivity and personalization.

Recommendations for adaptive and personalized environments

To alleviate some of the problems that adaptive and personalized environments bring, there are a number of recommendations that can be applied to solve those problems. One of the very basic recommendations is to provide students means to deactivate or limit the adaptation process. This can be done by providing students with a choice of whether they want adaptation in the learning environment or not. If a student is finding the adaptation mechanism distracting from their learning process, then the student should be able to either deactivate or limit its application to certain parts of the environment. Also, adaptation can be offered to students in the form of a proposal. Rather than applying the adaptation directly, the environment can monitor the student, identify what kind of adaptivity and personalization is needed for that student, and then ask the student whether he/she would like that kind of adaptivity and personalization. The environment can provide details of what would happen due to that particular adaptation and what will be the changes in the behaviour and interface of the environment. That would enable students to make informed choices.

Adaptive and personalized learning environments can also enable students to define specific parameters for adaptation. So, a student can say, "I want adaptation based on my learning styles but not based on my competence"; or, "I want adaptation in this particular chapter but not in another chapter", and so on. Also, giving students information about the effects of adaptation would prevent the surprise that students may get because of sudden modifications in the learning environment's interface. Another possibility to reduce the problems of adaptivity and personalization is for students to be able to select the content, such as simulation, for which the environment should provide adaptation and for which it should not. So, there are a number of ways in which learning environments can reduce the problems that may be caused due to adaptivity and personalization.

Another area of interest is the editable user model. Learning environments provide adaptivity and personalization based on what they monitor and what they infer about the student, and then what analysis they do out of that data. It is possible that because of errors in algorithm or simply because students change their behaviour during learning process, the analysis made by the environment may be incorrect. Therefore it should be possible for students to check what information the environment has about them, and if they find that some information is not correct, they should then be able to correct that information. However, this issue is like a double-edged sword. On one hand, if the environment has some wrong information, then correcting that information by the student would improve the effectiveness and efficiency of the adapativity and personalization mechanism. On the other hand, because the environment acquires information by monitoring the student, it is possible that the student may have misconceptions about his/her competency, and his/her preferences, and therefore, the student may change the information to something that is not a true representation of the student's attitude, his/her competency, or other characteristics. Therefore, whatever adaptation and personalization will take place from then on, would in fact, be an incorrect outcome, and chances are that the students' learning process will be hindered by the adaptivity and personalization. That would result in an improper learning process, unlike what is expected through adaptivity and personalization.

Levels of adaptivity and personalization

Depending on the situation, there are different levels of adaptivity and personalization that can be implemented in a learning environment. They can range from system based adaptivity, to different kinds of parameters and user characteristics that can be monitored in order to provide adaptivity.

More complex adaptive and personalized environments use context of the learning, and context of the situation.

For example, Browne, Totterdell and Norman (1990) identified four levels of adaptation based on the complexity of the representations maintained by the environment and the ability of the environment to utilize those representations. The first level includes 'simple' adaptive environments that use 'hard wired' rules, where depending on those rules, if a threshold is met, adaptivity and personalization kicks in. The second level is 'self-regulating', where the environment does the adaptation and then checks the effect of that adaptation, and if adaptation is not working properly, it changes the system behaviour again. The third level they identify is the 'self-mediating', where the environment identifies what needs to be adapted. It first puts the resulting adaptation on a model and then if everything looks good on the model, it brings it into practice with the student. The final level is 'self-modifying' adaptation, where the environment identifies what needs to be adapted, and then finds reasons about whether that adaptation is really necessary, what are the costs involved, and whether the benefits are worth the cost. Based on that, it does the adaptation.

Test your understanding

1. Please give three examples of how adaptivity and personalization mechanism can improve learning process in a learning environment.
2. How can adaptive and personalized learning environments help teachers in improving learning experiences of students in large classrooms?
3. What problems can occur due to the fact that learning environments need to monitor student actions to be able to provide adaptivity and personalization?
4. What is social monitoring and how can adaptive and personalized learning environments suffer from it?

A representative scenario

Here is a representative scenario for how adaptivity and personalization mechanism would work in a learning environment. When a student comes to the learning environment for the first time, the environment will check whether the student is registered or not. If the student is not registered, then the environment will try to find as much information about the student's background as possible. That would include the student's demographic details, such as whether the student is from an urban area or a rural community, and what kind of economic background the student is coming from. It will also try to find things like the student's learning style. There are lots of different models out there for learning styles and depending on the designer of the environment, a certain model will be used to identify a student's learning style. Student's mental abilities can also be checked, for example working memory capacity, which allows for keeping a limited amount of information active for a short time for mental processing, associative learning skill which is the skill to associate new concepts with previously learned concepts; inductive reasoning ability which is the ability to infer concepts from examples; information processing speed which is how quickly students can process certain information correctly; and many other such mental abilities which the environment can identify so that adaptivity and personalization can take place based on that information.

Then the environment will also try to identify what the student already knows about the domain content covered in the learning environment. For that, certain pretests or quizzes could be used to identify a student's current state of competence in that particular subject domain.

Once the environment has identified all these items, then based on that, the environment will determine what content to present to the student based on the student's competency, in what format to present it based on the student's learning styles, and what changes should be made to navigation, presentation and interaction, based on the mental abilities and other demographic details that the student has provided. Based on the demographic details, the environment can also select certain case studies that would work better for the student's background.

In an online learning environment where a student is just using a computer to learn, there may be certain limitations to what kind of skills can be provided to the student. But if the student would be learning outside in the physical world, that would open up more opportunities for learning different types of skills by combining real life objects with online information to provide more contextual and authentic learning. However, that would also increase the complexity of adaptivity and personalization because now the environment also has to take care of the student's location, what kind of devices the student is using, in what kind of situation the student is in, and other similar parameters.

So coming back to the previous scenario, once the student starts to learn, the environment will monitor how the student is performing, and whether the student has preference for some type of media. For example, the student is accessing more videos compared to looking at images or reading the text. Then it monitors how the student is performing after each unit. Even within a unit, certain small exercises could be given that will allow the adapativity and personalization mechanism to know more about the student's ongoing performance, and based on that, customize the content, in terms of its pre-sentation, navigation and possible interactions—all these aspects of the learning experience according to the student's continued evidence of performance. Similarly, the environment will identify if there are any changes in the student's learning styles or in the student's affective state, and based on that, the system will dynamically customize the content and behaviour of the learning environment to suit an individual student's needs.

So this is the kind of scenario which has a number of different input parameters from a student's characteristics. The learning environment takes these parameters into account to analyse what kind of adaptivity and personal-ization should take place, and, accordingly, provides presentation of the learning content, navigation, interaction possibilities, and other aspects of the learning environment.

Learning activities

1. Select a subject topic of your choice and select content that is more suitable for students who have high working memory capacity compared to those who have low working memory capacity.
2. Add more content to the content you created in the first activity so that the revised content provides adequate learning to the students with both high and low working memory capacities.
3. Identify what parts of the content created in the second activity you can remove so that the content remains suitable for the students with low working memory capacity but no longer serves for the students with high working memory capacity.

Share your ideas with your colleagues and ask them to critique. Provide feedback to your colleagues on their ideas in return.

Resources

User Modeling, Adaptation and Personalization: www.um.org

International Artificial Intelligence in Education Society: www.iaied.org

Journal of Educational Technology & Society: www.ifets.info

References

Browne, D.P., Totterdell, P.A., & Norman, M.A. (1990). *Adaptive User Interfaces*, London: Academic Press.

Hannafin M. J. & Peck K. L. (1988). *The Design, Development, and Evaluation of Instructional Software*. New York: Macmillan Publishing Company.

Oppermann R. (1994). Introduction. In Oppermann R. (Ed.), *Adaptive User Support*, Hillsdale, NJ: Lawrence Erlbaum Associates, pp1–13.

Oppermann R., Rashev R., & Kinshuk (1997). Adaptability and Adaptivity in Learning Systems. In A. Behrooz (Ed.), *Knowledge Transfer (volume II)*, London: Pace, 173–179 (ISBN 1–900427–015–X).

two
Adaptivity and Personalization in Life-Long Learning

Who uses adaptive and personalized learning environments? How are these environments different from face-to-face environment? Adaptive and personalized learning environments are typically used either as complementary resources to the face-to-face teaching or in online education where there are no experts available at the time students are learning. Since these environments are used by the students in their own time, at their own pace, from and wherever they are learning, it is impossible to guarantee that there will be an expert available to support learning at that particular moment. Many of these scenarios constitute life-long learning. Let us first look at what life-long learning is before discussing how people undertaking life-long learning can be supported by adaptivity and personalization.

Life-long learning consists of various forms of education, including formal, informal and non-formal education. Formal learning activities are those activities that are undertaken in a formal academic environment, typically a school or college or university, with a set curriculum and certain formal assessment procedures such as midterms or final exams. Non-formal activities are those that are not taught as part of the curriculum but they help students in their qualifications. They are done by the students in their own time, outside of the classroom without the help of the teacher, but the aim is to improve the skills and knowledge of what is prescribed in the syllabus. Informal learning activities are those learning activities that do not have learning as the main aim. They happen spontaneously, they can happen wherever there is an opportunity without previously identifying them as learning opportunities.

Life-long learning and life-long learners

Nowadays, students typically engage in formal, non-formal and informal learning activities regularly. Therefore learning is not anymore confined within the boundaries of academic institution, it can be argued that life-long learning happens even during student life. For example, students use Internet to search learning materials, use social media to interact with others, and various types of resources that are beyond the traditional academic environment. All these additional activities are included in life-long learning. But the problem with life-long learning is that it requires discipline on the part of the student. There is no teacher or expert sitting beside the student and telling what to do, when life-long learning takes place. That means, the motivation has to come from the student. The student must have desire to learn. There may be an intrinsic goal, such as, "I have to solve this problem in my work", but there has to be some motivation on the part of the student to explore the material, and he/she has to do it on his or her own initiative. When a teacher or expert is not present, which generally happens in such scenarios, then how will the student learn? Learning in such scenarios happens by observation—by reading something or watching something. For example, in office environment, the life-long learners may watch over the shoulder of a colleague doing a task and then try to do that task himself or herself. Observation and imitation are therefore key activities in life-long learning. In that sense, one can say that life-long learning actually starts from birth, since children learn in the same way. They watch parents, other elders, and other children in their surroundings and copy what they observe.

Life-long learning happens all the time. It can happen during student life and beyond, it continues after students graduate and move on to their work life, as and when there is a need for learning, and a need to have newer skills because of changes in the environment or technology. In such environments, learning happens because of a particular need, because life-long learning is something students do when they encounter any need to learn more. Motivation to learn is typically problem focused, because as and when students encounter any problem, they try to solve it, and at that moment they need certain knowledge and skills. So, that kind of learning also exhibits the same characteristics as life-long learning at adult age.

Nowadays, everyone has become a life-long learner since in today's environment, we learn about the things we need when we need them. The learning process has become very needs specific. What it means is, there is very little motivation for learning those concepts where relevance and usefulness to one's needs is not clear. This creates problems for abstract concepts. Many times it is difficult to explain why they are useful. For life-long learners, it is even more difficult, because if they do not see the use of it, so they do not put time for them. Then what happens is that they need to learn them when the need arises suddenly, just in time, or learning on demand. For example, such learning takes place in office environment or in the student's own environment. Such learning has become even more important in recent years since due to rapid changes in technology, the ways of doing things have been changing very fast. For example, some of us will remember the days of typewriters, where one mistake could mean typing a whole document again. We have come a long way since then, with sophisticated word processors that not only allow mistake corrections any time, but also help with auto-correction features and grammar suggestions. However, the more sophistication these word processors bring in, the more there is need for people to update their skills to use these word processor applications effectively. Before, we had piles of papers, but the technology nowadays provides us with a way to store the things electronically, and retrieve them hundreds of years later without losing a single bit, without losing quality and without losing any functionality of it. But in such environments where technology is evolving so fast, people have to update their skills frequently, and update them very fast. Otherwise, they get obsolete. The only way to keep up with the new demands of the jobs for most people is to learn through life-long learning. People do not have contact with subject experts during life-long learning, which is why many computer-based learning environments are coming into picture. What these environments can do? They are supposed to fill the gap between what human teachers could provide and what life-long learners need, without the experts. A lot of technology is coming up which can help people learn certain parts of domain competence in the absence of experts. Before discussing what kind of domain competence these environments are good at providing, let us look at various components of domain competence

Constituents of domain competence

Domain competence includes conceptual knowledge and skills. Skills can be divided into two kinds: cognitive decision making skills and operational hands-on skills. One way to look at domain competence is to consider a combination of conceptual knowledge and skills for different orientations (Figure 2.1).

The two basic orientations are know-how and know-why. Know-how is operational. It consists of competence required for action oriented tasks. These kinds of tasks can be done physically and one can observe how something is done. For example, someone wants to make a table. He/she can watch another person to see how it is done and then imitate that. By repetition and practice, one can achieve mastery in this type of competence. Know-how is therefore action-driven and experiential in nature. It is difficult to inherit this type of knowledge from someone else's experience. A number of visualization

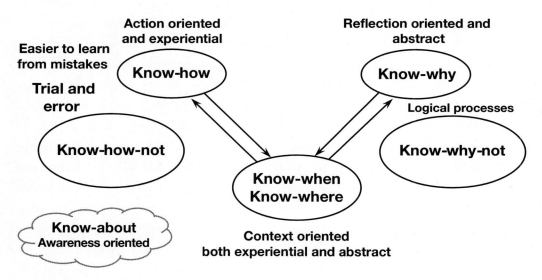

FIGURE 2.1 Components of domain competence

technologies can be used in computer-based learning environments to facilitate know-how, for example, videos and animations. Another aspect of know-how is its negation know-how-not. It represents the type of experiential learning where students can learn by making mistakes realising that the goal is not achieved through the learning paths that were erroneously adopted. If you did something and it did not work out, then you know that this is not how it should be done. This is an important part of operational learning and students who are afraid to make mistakes have to undergo a longer learning cycle. This type of learning is so important that in case of critical or hazardous systems, computer simulation and virtual reality are increasingly being employed. In such disastrous and dangerous scenarios, such as learning about nuclear reactors, simulations and virtual reality can enable students to manipulate various parameters and test the outcomes to understand what works and what not. So one can learn by mistakes.

Know-why, on the other hand, is about understanding the reasoning behind certain concepts and relationships. It requires reflection on the part of the student and therefore provides abstract learning. Know-how can be inherited from other people's explanations, following their line of reasoning, provided there is effective communication. The negation aspect of know-why is know-why-not, which seems to logically follow from know-why rather than other way around. It is still possible to learn from mistakes but this requires a much deeper reflection. It is very difficult to learn the correct reasoning just by looking at the reasons of why something is not correct. It requires deeper reflection and a lot of thinking. It is challenging to provide know-why and know-why-not through computers. Say, if you have to explain, you must have a reasoning. Someone can explain to you that this is why that thing is done. That is easy. But learning requires reflection and asking explanations. When you want to provide your arguments or counteract someone else's reasoning, then the other person should be capable of understanding your reasoning. Now replace that other person with a computer. The first requirement is then natural language processing, which is still not yet advanced enough to understand different nuances of academic dialogue and has not yet been able to understand the different contexts that even a four year old child can do. So, for know-why and know-why-not aspects, computers are not able to adequately complement human teachers. Further critical components of know-why and know-why-not include non-verbal cues, effect of tone, and use of contextual elements that are present in human conversations and significantly influence the dialogue. For example, while conversing, people watch their counterparts to try to figure out whether the other person following their reasoning, agreeing or disagreeing, or other effects, and they change their explanations and ways of talking as needed Computers do not yet have that capability. While research on sentiment analysis and emotions has picked the interest of many researchers, it is nowhere near to being useful in academic conversations. For example, people sometime use positively sounding words with a negative tone (e.g., "yyeeaahh"). What would that mean? For a computer, that would be a "Yes", and it will go ahead. A human will know that this "yyeeaahh" actually had different meaning and he/she will react accordingly. Computers will not do that.

The application of know-how and know-why are also influenced by the location and time context. Know-where represents location context whereas know-when provides time-based contextual orientation. For know-how, for example, a sequence of operations—when something needs to be done, may be different at different times. In know-why, the reasoning may be required why something needs to be done at a particular moment. Organizational policies as well as other environmental factors may also impose these contextual constraints. Know-where implies, where something needs to be done, influencing know-how. It may also require reasoning, the "why" component—the explanation component. So, know-when and know-where are the contextual orientation of both know-how and know-why.

Next comes know-about. It is about awareness. What the students already know and what they do not know. If a student is aware that there are parts of domain knowledge and skills that he/she does not even know about but that they exist, that is awareness, and is encompassed in know-about. It includes all domain competence in it whether already acquired by a student or not. Basically the environmental context comes in picture.

Test your understanding

1. What is the difference between know-how and know-why?
2. Why is it more difficult to learn from know-why-not compared to know-how-not?
3. What components of domain competence are included in know-about?

Instruction in knowledge context

So, then, how about computers? Where do they fit? What computers can do? Which components of know-how, know-why, know-when, know-where and know-about computers can handle very well?

Let us take a practical example of simple mathematics. How could computers be used to show how to add a list of numbers? You can provide observation. You can create a wizard, which shows a cursor going from one place, clicking on, say, the formula button, clicking on the sum, and then dragging from one cell to another, to select the range, and then clicking on the destination cell to get the sum. One can observe it, and can then repeat it to learn. You can provide animation of it and you can provide simulation of it, and provide lots of parameters which people can change and can learn, how sum cannot be done, how the mistakes can be made. If they make mistakes, and the result is not what they expected, they learn.

Let us try another example: why the coral reefs on New Zealand coast are blue? Try to teach it with a computer and then try to argue with it. Computer technologies are not yet evolved sufficiently to provide reasoning based learning with open-ended arguments. Therefore, computers are not yet able to provide know-why components adequately. Know-when and know-where require contextual understanding, which is even more complicated to provide through typical computer systems.

Computers are, however, very good in visualization, in providing facilities for observation and experimentation. They have extensive multimedia capabilities. And therefore, they are good for know-how. Know-why, on the other hand, requires natural language interaction. Besides, with different cultural and geographical connotations, different metaphors come in picture. And that is another place where computers are not yet suitable. Creating a user model to know who this user is works only with the assumption that I am sitting here, logged in as me and using the system with no other thing on my mind. I can go for a cup of coffee and system will think that I am incompetent in reading a page in an amount of time deemed sufficient for such page. That is what computers do, because that is what they are programed to do. They do not understand metaphors, because metaphors require cultural upbringing. Metaphors require that human aspect which computers do not (yet) have.

In know-how, you do the things, you show the things. It is visualization. What I shall argue is how it relates to cognitive skills, since cognitive skills are something you cannot show. Hypermedia based systems try to provide the kind of learning needed for cognitive skills, through explanations and non-linear structure facilitated through links, but these systems are not instructional systems themselves. Hypermedia systems are a collection of resources. They provide wonderful exploration possibilities as long as the students are motivated to learn and have the skills to explore non-linear content structure that hypermedia provides. These systems act more like a librarian who can provide various resources on demand, but the demand has to come from the student. Hypermedia on its own does not have teaching capability. It also does not have any built-in intelligent guidance. Separate adaptivity and personalization mechanisms are needed to support the learner, where hypermedia systems can act as content repository. However, hypermedia systems do a good job of motivating students to move further. Since these systems contain links, they provide information at varying granularity, and provoke the students to follow through those links to know more about certain topics.

With emergence of mobile devices, it is now slowly becoming possible to also provide the context of know-when and know-where. Most of the mobile phones are nowadays equipped with GPS sensors that can not only precisely identify the student's location in real time but also track the movement history to create patterns of student's learning process in physical environment. This can serve as the basis for providing basic adaptivity for know-where component of the domain competence. By tracking the time for each of student's actions on the mobile device, the learning environment can also create profile of student's action in the context of various learning activities. It is also possible to check student activity in various other learning environments, such as learning management systems, by analyzing timestamps in the log files. It is therefore also becoming possible for the adapativity and personalization mechanism to start to customize learning experience for know-when component of the domain competence. In a later chapter, we shall look at some of the frameworks and implementations that attempt to provide underlying support for these different components of domain competence.

Test your understanding

1. Why are computers more suitable for know-how than know-why?
2. What characteristics of know-why make it difficult to be taught by computers?

Learning activities

1. Identify three ways in which computers can provide effective learning for know-how component of domain competence? Share them with your colleagues and ask them to providing a critique. Critique one or more of their maps in exchange for the feedback.
2. Select a topic of your choice and identify one activity each for know-how and know-why. Explain how those activities could be taught through computers.
3. Develop a scenario of a subject topic of your choice where the time of day affects the learning process (hint: certain processes happen only in the day). Share your findings with your colleagues and ask them if they would have come to the same conclusion. Reflect on their feedback by comparing your findings with their views. Give your colleagues feedback on their findings in return.

Links

Life-long learning: http://en.wikipedia.org/wiki/Lifelong_learning

Intelligent tutoring systems: http://en.wikipedia.org/wiki/Intelligent_tutoring_system

Sentiment analysis: http://en.wikipedia.org/wiki/Sentiment_analysis

Additional readings

Fakinlede, I., Kumar, V., & Wen, D. (2013). Knowledge Representation for Context and Sentiment Analysis. Proceedings of the 2013 IEEE 13th International Conference on Advanced Learning Technologies, Los Alamitos, CA: IEEE Computer Society, 493–494.

Kinshuk (2002). Cognitive Skills Acquisition in Life-long Learning (Part 1). *Interactive Learning Environments*, 10 (2), 89–91.

Kinshuk (2003). Cognitive Skills Acquisition in Life-long Learning (Part 2). *Interactive Learning Environments*, 11 (1), 1–2.

Lin, T., & Kinshuk (2009). Cognitive profiling in life-long learning. In P. Rogers, G. Berg, J. Boettcher, C. Howard, L. Justice, & K. Schenk (Eds.), Encyclopedia of Distance Learning (2nd Ed.), Hershey, PA: Information Science Reference., 295–305.

three
Contexts

Success of learning is influenced by the context in which it is taking place. It is therefore important to understand how context affects adaptivity and personalization. We shall look at the application of context in learning environments that support adaptivity and personalization. Research on contexts emerged from different perspectives. Context is basically a situation in which certain things happen. Context could be environment. Context could be the communication. Context could be different types of knowledge that are applicable in certain circumstances. So, context has wider meaning. In intelligent environments in general, there has been lot of research on the use of context in knowledge management, in reasoning, and in natural language processing, because in these areas, answers to questions are different in different contexts. For example, in natural language processing, the same sentence can have different meaning in different languages. Taking English and Chinese, there is a huge difference between how people understand certain things, and if you try to translate a sentence from Chinese to English, a direct translation may not work. One has to actually understand the meaning before attempting the translation, otherwise the meaning will be completely different. So, context plays a very significant role in these environments.

Role of context in adaptive and personalized learning

In adaptive and personalized learning environments, where students access computer systems from anywhere in the world through the Internet, depending on the situation, depending on who the student is, and depending on the objectives of the instruction and the pedagogy, context makes a big difference. Research on context in adaptive and personalized learning environments has targeted various areas, such as knowledge representation—how to present knowledge to the student; discourse management—how the dialog happens with the student, how students discuss concepts with each other and with the teacher, and in what environment they do it; and, other architectural aspects to improve student–computer interaction and how to provide effective tutoring strategies. The same student in different situations will need different types of learning. How can one decide that since today the student is learning a topic for the first time, we should provide him/her perhaps more detailed content; and, then, just before the exam, the student should be provided only summarized content for revision? What criteria one should use to decide all that? There has been research on using context for taking these decisions.

An important issue to consider is that until now, the application of context or implementation of context has been only inside the computer-based learning environments, because most of the time, when we talk about adaptive and personalized learning environments, people generally think in terms of computer systems. So, the focus remains on something that is happening inside the computer, which can be programmed. But context plays much wider role. Context also has role in how people perceive certain things; in what situations such adaptive and personalized environments should be used. From that perspective, context plays a much wider role than just inside the computer systems.

Types of contexts

Let us look at different types of contexts that are within the computer systems and outside the computer systems. Context can be classified into three categories: interactional context, objectival context, and environmental context (see Figure 3.1).

Interactional context plays a role between the computer-based learning environment and the student. This type of context is what people typically think about when considering applications of context in online learning systems. This context is relevant when a student is using an adaptive and personalized learning environment. The interaction in this case is between the student and the computer system.

However, this interaction between the student and the environment is also affected by the teaching process (the pedagogy favored and used by the teacher) and the assessment process (how the assessment will take place). Many students learn simply to pass the exam. Even when they want to learn something with interest, the main goal for the majority of students still remains passing the exam. The learning process therefore is very much shaped by the nature of the exam, how teachers view the exam, and what kind of learning activities a teacher has provided in the learning environment. So, the interaction between the environment and the student is affected by the teaching process and assessment process. This context is called **objectival context**. Objectival context looks at the objective of learning.

Furthermore, the whole process of learning, teaching and assessment is affected by the situation in which the learning is taking place, for example, what

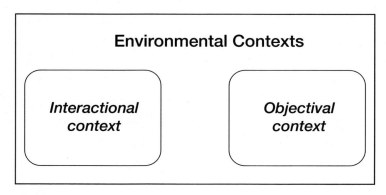

FIGURE 3.1 Types of contexts

are the university policies, and what are the employment prospects in the country. There are a multitude of contexts that affect the learning process from outside, and are therefore very important when designing adaptive and personalized learning environments. These contexts are called **environmental contexts**.

Interactional context: This type of context is between the student and the computer-based learning environment. Consideration of this context by adaptivity and personalization helps in improving the communication between the computer and the user—typically known as human-computer interaction. The better the learning environment understands the student, the more the environment knows about the student, the better the communication will be and the environment will be able to provide more intelligent feedback to the student. The environment will be able to provide customized and personalized feedback to the student.

Similarly, it is quite important for the student to know about the capabilities of the learning environment, because the environments are designed to do certain tasks and have their limitations. The better appreciation the student has about what the environment can or cannot do, the more realistic the expectations will be from the student about the environment. This will avoid any unnecessary frustration on the part of the student that may arise if the student expects something that the environment is not capable of doing.

Application of interactional context can be found in various types of learning environments, such as intelligent tutoring systems, and adaptive and personalized learning environments. They are typically represented in plan recognition—what the student wants to learn; knowledge structuring—what kind of knowledge the student's needs—which units, which topics, and at what depth; knowledge representation—how to best present the knowledge to the student, and in what format; reasoning—understanding the student's thinking process through his/her responses—instead of simply pointing out the mistakes the student made, inferring the misconceptions or missing conceptions the student may have that caused the mistakes he/she made; and discourse management—analyzing the dialogue between the student and the learning environment, the student and the teacher, and among the students, and identifying the most effective ways to facilitate the discussions.

Environmental context: There are a number of factors that contribute to environmental contexts (Patel et al., 1998):

i. Students: Different students have different capabilities, preferences, learning styles, motivation for learning, and competencies in the content being learned, which affect how they approach learning while interacting with the learning environments. Also, learning generally does not happen in isolation. Students may work in groups or simply interact with other students in online learning, and gain knowledge outside of the learning environment. Adaptive and personalized learning environments also need to take into account such interactions with peers, considering the capabilities, preferences, learning styles, motivation, competencies and other personal attributes of those peers, and how they affect the student's learning process.

ii. Teachers: In formal learning scenarios, teachers play a very important role. Typically, students in formal learning will use primarily those learning resources and environments that their teacher has recommended or asked to use. So, teachers' preferences and outlook affect the learning process. Similarly, a negative recommendation from a teacher will likely result in the majority of students not using a certain resource or environment. This is not so different from the scenario where teachers use certain books in their classes. Those books are authored by someone else, typically an expert in the discipline, who may even be from another country. Teachers generally ask students to use the book but leave out, for example, certain case studies because those case studies do not have any local relevance, or an example, because the example is from different culture and does not have any meaning for the current students. The teacher then provides his/her own case studies and examples that are contextually relevant, while still using the book for other parts. The same applies to the learning environments. These environments are designed by someone else, and they are used by students elsewhere under the recommendation and guidance of their local teacher. Teachers' preferences and outlook therefore significantly influence the learning process.

iii. Discipline: The nature of the discipline influences the learning practices. Different disciplines require students to learn various aspects at different granularity levels, and as disciplines mature, they inherit complexities and semantic that is known and understood only within that discipline. Over time, disciplines evolve their own terminology which has an established meaning within that discipline, and the same words may have completely different meaning outside of that discipline. For example, the word "cloud" has specific meaning in technological disciplines, while it may be understood differently from people outside. For a novice student, who is not yet familiar with such discipline specifics, the adaptive and personalized environments would need to only provide the basic content. However, as the student progresses, the learning environment will need to ensure that in addition to the content, the student is also becoming aware of those discipline-specific nuances for effective learning experience.

iv. Knowledge: Different types of knowledge require different treatment for effective learning. For example, in applied disciplines, such as science and engineering, there is a lot of visual content and there are lots of hands-on activities. In contrast, in disciplines such as history and philosophy, the content is primarily textual and there is more reflection and analysis. Adaptive and personalized learning environments will therefore need to provide different learning experience to the students based on the needs of the discipline. So, for the student learning philosophy, the environment will need to provide lots of opportunities for reflection through textual discussions, blogs and other similar means. On the other hand, for a student learning a topic in science, system would need to visualize content through animations, images, and other visual items and provide various hands-on activities through simulations, image maps and other media resources that provide opportunities for action.

v. Medium: The capabilities of the device used by the students to access the learning environment also have significant influence on the learning experience of the students. Similarly, different technological affordances have direct impact on the learning process. What kind of hardware is available? What kind of processing it can do? What kind of software capabilities it has? What kinds of communication options are possible? Are audio and video communication channels available? Is it possible to type text? For example, if the device is not able to render certain type of media and the course content available in the learning environment is primarily in that media, it can have significant negative effect on the learning experience. Mobile devices are particularly prone to this issue, such as, Apple devices, as iPhones and iPads do not support Adobe Flash. In such situation, despite all the interactivity that Adobe Flash provides, students will be unable to learn anything if they have only Apple devices available. Another characteristic of the medium is bandwidth. Is there enough bandwidth available to download big multimedia files? If the student is using a low bandwidth connection and the content demands viewing videos, then the student will keep waiting for long time for the files to download before any learning can happen!

vi. Social environment: Different societal norms affect learning. Some behaviours and ideas that are very acceptable in one society may not be seen appropriate in another. The same is true for different academic institutions whose students would be using a particular learning environment. Different institutions have different policies and traditions. Since adaptive and personalized learning environments are expected to be used by students from different parts of the world, they need to serve the needs of heterogeneous student population and ensure that students do not misunderstand the inherent meaning that the teacher intended. Such misunderstandings can happen not only due to cultural differences but also economic, professional and other characteristics of the society a particular student is coming from. Different societies use different metaphors to explain different phenomenon. A simple example would be the use of word "recycle bin" in technology that is used to indicate a place where you can put some electronic document that you do not need anymore but do not want to completely discard in case it may be needed in future. The metaphor of recycle bin is inherited from the actual basket many of us have at home or office where we put items that may be reused later. If one deletes everything from recycle bin on the computer, it cannot be recovered again. This is similar to emptying the recycle basket in real world, where once the contents are thrown in garbage, they cannot be retrieved again. While there is no direct connection between the uses in real world and electronic world, the common understanding of the word in real world makes it easier to understand the concept in technology. Therefore the environment needs to make sure that the presentation of learning content and explanations are making sense to individual students. While more complex analysis of students' backgrounds and other characteristics can provide the environment with a better understanding of a student's perspective, just providing content through multiple formats and examples could go long way to support the needs of diverse students.

Objectival context: This context relates to the learning and teaching process. These processes are mainly concerned with how we teach in a classroom in comparison to how an adaptive and personalized learning environment is expected to teach. A traditional syllabus consists of all the subject knowledge that is considered essential and a teacher endeavors to cover as much of the syllabus as possible. The teaching model is thus implicitly based on a model of 'perfect' knowledge.

Teachers in the classroom typically focus on providing sound understanding of the overall subject matter and do not generally cover the whole prescribed syllabus for the course. Then, the assessment procedures, such as exams, do not try to assess 100% of what has been covered in the classroom, and more so, the students are not expected to perform 100% in exams to successfully complete the course. So, the assessment methods employed may only cover 60% to 80% of the syllabus and a student performance of a 50% score may indicate a pass mark. Thus a 30% to 40% proven knowledge of the syllabus indicates acceptable knowledge i.e., assessment methods implicitly accept 'imperfection' (Figure 3.2).

While this is a quite acceptable and established process in traditional educational systems, the expectations from online learning environments remain quite different. These environments are expected to impart mastery in the students for 100% coverage of the subject content. Designing adaptive and personalized learning environments therefore requires a thorough

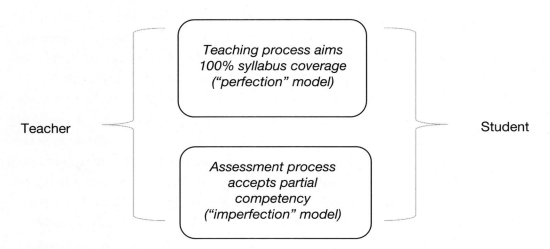

FIGURE 3.2 "Perfection" and "imperfection" model of learning and assessment

consideration of the objectives of traditional education and the anomaly when it comes to the expectations with the learning environments. Such consideration would look at the objectives of the learning and the need to cover the body of knowledge that is growing in all disciplines. Focus on meta-learning skills, such as problem solving, critical thinking, reflection and analytical skills will not only provide a justification to move away from the need to provide mastery in every component of the subject content but will also prepare students with 21st century skills that are essential in today's society.

Reflection

- Is the objective of traditional education to encourage acquisition of the facts and rules constituting the knowledge of a discipline or is it to encourage acquisition of meta-learning abilities? Please support your perspective with justification and examples.
- Should an adaptive and personalized learning environment encourage acquisition of meta-learning abilities? If yes, how? If not, why not?

A representative scenario

Adaptive and personalized learning environments are designed by some-one and used by someone else. Typically, the designer team of such learning environments has content experts, who have their own experience and per-spective of the discipline and subject content, and have their own ideas about the student expectations. These experts may have their own teaching style and personality attributes but they are also aware of various other teaching styles and personality attributes that the teachers recommending their environment to students worldwide may possess.

These learning environments are then used by the students under the guidance of a local teacher who is also a subject expert and has his/her teaching style and personality attributes. He/she is also aware of the particular needs of his/her students. If the local teacher finds the learning environment useful but at the same time perceives some components of the learning environment not matched with his/her teaching style or personality attributes, he/she would recommend the students to use the rest of the environment except those components. The task of identifying what components of the environment are going to be useful for his/her students would be easier for the local teacher if there was a mechanism available to reflect the teaching style and personality attributes of the designer teacher. The adaptivity and personalization mechanism of the learning environment can play a significant role by maintaining teacher model of the designer teacher, and creating similar teacher model of the local teachers, and then comparing them to identify alignments and mismatches.

Looking at the interaction between a student and the learning environment, this interaction is influenced by several external forces that an adaptivity and personalization mechanism needs to take into account. The two actors, the learning environment and the student have their own characteristics. The student has certain types of natural abilities, such as working memory capacity, associative learning skills, etc. The student also has certain types of learning styles. He/she also has specific motivation for learning. In addition, the student, being an intelligent person in general, also has specific perspective about the capabilities of the learning environment and corresponding expectations from that learning environment.

The learning environment, on the other hand, is designed by a content expert and therefore reflects the teaching style and perspectives of that designer expert. Designer expert also has certain perspectives about what a learning environment, which will be used by different students and teachers worldwide, should be. In addition, that expert also has certain perspective about the needs and expectations of those teachers who will recommend the environment to their students. The learning environment therefore enables the designer expert to indirectly influence the interaction between the student and the learning environment.

The student is also learning through the learning environment in a scenario that is guided by his/her local teacher. The local teacher has his/her teaching style and certain perspective about how a learning environment should function. So, the student is learning under a complex interplay of various perspectives, expectations and styles that shape the learning experience. The adaptivity and personalization mechanism of the learning environment needs to consider all these aspects to ensure effective learning (see Figure 3.3).

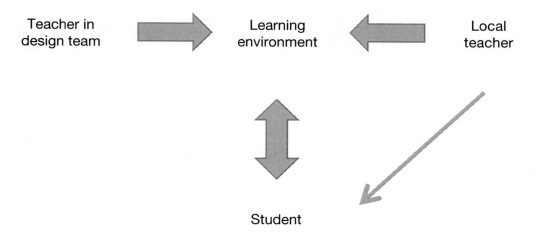

FIGURE 3.3 Application of contexts in learning environments

Test your understanding

1. What is the most common use of context in learning environments?
2. What is the difference between "perfection" and "imperfection" models of learning and assessment?
3. Why is it important to consider the teaching styles and perspectives of the teacher who is in the designer team?

Learning activities

1. Create a concept map of various environmental contexts to show how they relate to each other. Share the map with your colleagues and ask them to provide a critique. Critique one or more of their maps in exchange for the feedback.
2. Develop a scenario of a subject topic of your choice where different teacher teach the topic differently. Identify how the teaching styles of different teachers would impact the learning process of the students. Share your findings with your colleagues and ask them if they would have come to the same conclusion. Reflect on their feedback by comparing your findings with their views. Give your colleagues feedback on their findings in return.

Additional readings

Bazire, M., & Brézillon, P. (2005). Understanding Context Before Using It. *Lecture in Computer Science, 3554,* 29–40.

Zimmermann, A., Lorenz, A., & Oppermann, R. (2007). An Operational Definition of Context. *Lecture Notes in Computer Science, 4635,* 558–571.

References

Patel, A., Russell, D., Kinshuk, Oppermann, R. & Rashev, R. (1998). An initial framework of contexts for designing usable intelligent tutoring systems. *Information Services and Use,* 18 (1–2), 65–76 (ISSN 0167–5265).

part two

THEORETICAL PERSPECTIVES WITH EXAMPLE APPLICATIONS

four
Cognitive Profiling

Adaptive and personalized learning environments strive on supporting the learning process of students by understanding their competencies in the subject matter and their personal abilities to learn. One of the important characteristics that adaptive and personalized learning environments take into account is the cognitive abilities of the students. In this chapter, we shall look at various cognitive abilities that can affect the learning process and the concept of cognitive profiling which adaptive and personalized learning environments use to understand about students' cognitive abilities. We shall also see examples of how these environments can support students better by considering their cognitive abilities.

Cognitive abilities have been studied extensively in the area of cognitive psychology. There are a number of cognitive abilities (also called cognitive attributes) that affect learning process. In this chapter we shall look at some of these abilities and discuss how we can first measure them while students are learning in an adaptive and personalized learning environment, and then use that information to provide adaptivity and personalization. Cognitive abilities are related to the mind and not to the task a student is doing. This means that once a particular cognitive ability of a student has been measured, this information can be used by the environment to support a student in various subjects. The interesting thing is that it also does not matter what subject the student was studying when his/her cognitive ability was measured. Cognitive abilities can therefore be measured regardless of the subject matter a student is learning. They also tend to remain at same level for longer periods of time.

It is important for adaptive and personalized learning environments to consider cognitive abilities of individual students. If a student with a certain low cognitive ability encounters learning content or another aspect of the learning process that demands a higher level of that cognitive ability, the student may experience a lot of stress in performing that learning task or may even be forced to give up that task if the cognitive load becomes too high. On the other hand, if a student with high cognitive abilities encounters too simplistic learning material, he or she may become bored and lose motivation.

Examples of cognitive abilities

Let us look at some of the examples of cognitive abilities that affect learning processes of students. In particular, we shall discuss working memory capacity, associative learning skills and inductive reasoning ability.

Working memory capacity

Working memory ability allows humans to keep a limited amount of information active in the brain for a short period of time. It stores the results of intermediate calculations and computations when we solve any problem, and enables us to perform further computations on the intermediary results stored. Alan Baddeley has done extensive exploration of working memory capacity (see Baddeley, 1992 and 2000). Working memory affects speed of learning, memorisation of learned concepts, skills acquisition effectiveness and many other learning processes. Capacity of working memory primarily consists of a limited storage system and a central execution unit that carries out various mental operations. In the context of learning, the adaptivity and personalization mechanism mainly looks at working memory for synchronizing operation with the central execution unit for the formation of higher order rules, building up of the mental model and ensuring that the working memory storage system does not get overloaded in the process.

Working memory capacity used to be also known as short-term memory, due to its nature of storing information for short periods of time. However, it functions differently from the long-term memory that stores historical information for longer periods. It also includes a processing component which is known as Central Executive and is connected to fluid intelligence in people and provides an ability to think logically, identify patterns and solve problems in unfamiliar situations. The structure of working memory has been a matter of discussion for decades, and the consensus is that it can be described as a control-slave system that contains a central executive, which is the controlling and processing component, phonological loop, which is a slave component for verbal information, and a visual-spatial sketch-pad, which is another slave component for graphical information. The central executive monitors and controls the output of the phonological loop and the visual-spatial sketch-pad, and selects relevant parts for processing.

Both storage capacity and operation capacity of working memory are significant in terms of the process of students. Young adults have been found to have higher operational capacity than older adults. Speed of execution is another factor that affects the performance of working memory. However, the storage capacity and speed of execution do not exist in isolation. Higher storage capacity makes it easier for students to chunk concepts and relations into higher order or abstract units, which in turn have a positive effect on the speed of execution.

Working memory also acts as a gateway to allow information transfer into long-term memory. This requires channeling the information being received from various senses to the semantically networked structure of the long-term memory and includes various mental efforts such as interpretation, translation, association, memorisation, and so on. Students with more efficient working memory ability are therefore able to put better mental efforts and channel information to long-term memory more effectively.

Students who have holistic learning styles tend to have significantly lower short-term memory components of working memory capacity and better learning outcomes in the long run. These students tend to jump directly to complex concepts in their learning process instead of following the curriculum in a linear fashion. On the other hand, those students who have serialistic learning styles and are capable of following and remembering sequentially fixed information have higher short-term memory and poorer long-term learning outcomes. These students typically adopt linear navigational strategies and follow the learning content in the sequence as it is provided to them.

An important concept in the learning process is activation, where activation of one concept causes automatic activation of associated concepts from the long-term memory. The level of activation is affected by the number of associations activated, since the more associations there are to share the limited amount available for activations, the less each association can get. Only when the activation level is more than a certain threshold, the student can bring a concept to consciousness from long-term memory. The total amount of activation is dependent of the working memory, and therefore working memory capacity influences the process of bringing previously learnt concepts to consciousness (see OSPAN and Web-OSPAN for measuring working memory capacity's role in concept consciousness through attention switching method).

Working memory affects the control of attention as it affects the ability to ignore irrelevance or distraction. Students with high working memory capacity are able to control their attention better than those with low working memory capacity. Similarly, students with high working memory capacity are also able to resist distraction and focus on their learning goals better than their low working memory capacity counterparts. Interference is also a factor in the learning process which is affected by the level of working memory capacity. Interference happens when new items enter into working memory, existing items become harder to access, making the cognitive system less efficient. Students with low working memory capacity have low tolerance to interference.

Working memory capacity is task independent. It is important to consider that development of higher order presentation, for example, making a mental model of a concept, does reduce the load on working memory capacity; it is not a function of working memory itself. Another relation of working memory important in terms of the learning process is with field dependency. Field independent students are highly analytic and they operate with an internal frame of reference. These students prefer concrete learning material On the other hand, field-independent students operate with a relatively external frame of reference and process information globally. These students prefer to learn from abstract material. Students with high working memory capacity tend to be field-independent whereas those with low working memory capacity are more the field-dependent type.

Various learning activities of the students can give clues regarding the student's working memory capacity level. For example, a student who is slow when comparing two or more items, who is unable to complete long sequences of calculations without writing down intermediate results, or someone who has low resistance to interference, will likely have low working memory capacity. On the other hand, a student who learns in a leaner navigational pattern without a need to go back to previously learnt content, who exhibits high comparison speeds, who is able to retrieve information from long-term memory effectively, is likely to have high working memory capacity. Taiyu Lin provided an extensive list of these clues in his doctoral thesis (Lin, 2007). It is very important to understand that people may exhibit certain clues due to reasons other than their working memory capacity level. For example, a student who has high working memory capacity may still visit previously learnt content just because that student has habit of revising multiple times. Therefore, a single clue or just a few of the clues may not give sufficient evidence of a student's working memory capacity. However, the more number of clues point to the same level of working memory capacity, the more reliable the conclusion would be about the level of that student's working memory capacity.

Test your understanding

- List any three ways in which working memory capacity affects the learning process of students.
- Why is short-term memory name not sufficient for working memory capacity?
- Give two examples of clues that learning activities can provide for a student's working memory capacity level.

Inductive reasoning ability

Another cognitive ability that has significant influence on learning is inductive reasoning ability. It is the process of moving from concrete instances to generalization in human reasoning. Inductive reasoning has been regarded as one of the crucial mental abilities that is responsible for intelligent behaviour of humans. Inductive reasoning ability is also one of the best predictors of academic performance. It is therefore no surprise that it is has influence on problem solving, learning of concepts, learning of mathematics, and expertise development. On the other hand, inductive reasoning ability itself is influenced by the level of working memory capacity, ability of learning from analogies and ability to generate hypothesis.

In an adaptive and personalized learning environment, inductive reasoning ability can help students in transferring learning from one context to another. Students with high inductive reasoning ability are able to easily recognize the similarities and differences of various aspects in the current context and previously experienced contexts by filtering information, encoding it and classifying it. They can recognize and match patterns between the contexts by detecting co-variants from a list of examples encountered in past, and they can identify the theories and methods from looking at examples that incorporate those theories and methods. This is done by generating hypothesis and systematically deriving the rationale behind the hypothesis.

Inductive reasoning starts by data gathering activity, which includes collecting meaningful data, organizing it, and presenting it in a structured form so that inductive reasoning can be applied. The efficiency of inductive reasoning depends on how relevant and useful the collected data is. Students with high inductive reasoning ability are able to pinpoint relevant pieces of data faster and with ease. They do so not by hunch but through a broader sense of knowing what needs to done and by using previous experiences with something similar. These students are able to group items with similar attributes together effectively. High inductive reasoning ability students are also able to filter data that is relevant from the data that is not, and therefore arrive at the right conclusions better than those students who have low inductive reasoning ability.

Inductive reasoning ability has significant influence on transferability of learning, which is the ability to apply conceptual knowledge obtained from previously learnt procedural knowledge into new contexts. While new contexts need to be different from any previously experienced contexts, there have to be some similarities between them. Students with higher inductive reasoning ability will be able to induce and select a mental model that is appropriate for problem solving in the current context. This requires pattern matching to match the environmental variables that show the similarities between the two contexts. Pattern matching requires comparison, which is a mental process that requires high working memory capacity. Therefore students with high inductive reasoning ability tend to also have high working memory capacity.

Learning by analogy, where students use analogies or parallel concepts to initiate understanding of a concept that is being currently learnt, is affected by inductive reasoning ability. Analogies help students to see new situations using familiar and already experienced situations, since they provide a framework that is already structured in which students can receive information of the new situation. Metaphors also work as analogies and provide the similar familiarity. Students with higher inductive reasoning ability tend to learn better in such analogy based learning situations.

Inductive reasoning ability also influences the systematic thinking process of students where students use the process of elimination systematically from a list of possible solutions instead of merely guessing, hence increasing the efficiency of the learning process. It also affects the ability to find classifications that students use to understand higher order concepts by going through a set of examples. The more classifications a student can find from a set of examples, the more chances there are for the student to extract the right concept.

To be able to assess the level of students' inductive reasoning abilities, the adaptivity and personalization mechanism can use various clues students exhibit during their interactions with learning activities. For example, when a student shows poor ability to generalize when given many examples, when he/she does not undertake any activity to confirm a hypothesis at hand, or when the environment detects students as unable to learn from analogic learning content, it is highly likely that the student has low inductive reasoning ability. On the other hand, a student who demonstrates good systematic thinking, who is good at filtering relevant data from irrelevant data for a given problem, or who is able to easily learn from analogies, is likely to have high inductive reasoning ability. The more number of clues which point to the same level of inductive reasoning ability, the more reliable the conclusion would be about the level of that student's inductive reasoning ability.

Let us take an example of how an adaptive and personalized learning environment could support a student with low inductive reasoning ability. For such a student, the environment could increase the number of exploration paths, to give the student more opportunity to observe how concepts are applied in examples or are different from similar concepts. More stimulations of different contextual variables can promote inductive reasoning, and make the learning be more transferable to other contexts. The student can be given exploration paths of varying relevance so that the student can have more diverse observations in order to promote induction. The amount of information given to the student can be increased by giving detailed and step-by-step explanations so that the student can see the occurrences of pattern easily. The student can be provided with more structured information so that it is easier for the student to build up the mental model from the clues given in the structure of the information, despite low inductive reasoning ability. Similarly, the information can be more concrete and more examples and case studies can be provided to the student so that it is easier for him/her to generalize, leading to more transferable learning. The student can be provided with the information in a variety of formats to suit the learning style of the student, so that there is higher possibility that the concept to be learned can be associatively/analogically matched to a previously learned concept and hence increases the possibility for successful induction.

Learning activity

- Create a learning activity in a topic of your choice that uses analogy.

Associative learning skill

Associative learning skill enables students to associate newly learnt knowledge with previously learnt knowledge. Adaptive and personalized learning environments can customize the learning content and other aspects of the learning process to students to suit their associative learning skills in order to improve their learning experience. For example, for students with high associative learning skills, the environment can use previously learnt knowledge as examples and increase the opportunities for the students to learn from association. There are two aspects of associative learning that can affect students' learning processes. When students are shown the same concept in more than one example, they can start to see the links between those examples and actually change the way they behave towards working with those examples. The second aspect relates to students activating understanding of a new example because they suddenly remember a previous example and can see how those two examples are related. For students with high associative learning skills, the adaptivity and personalization mechanism can provide appropriate examples for students to take advantage of their high associative learning skills.

One specific aspect of associative learning skills that influences students' learning process is divergent associative learning skills. Divergent associative learning bring aspects of divergent thinking with associative learning, which enables students to create new associations between the new knowledge and previously learnt knowledge. It enables students to search suitable concepts from previously learnt knowledge that they can use to associate with new concepts.

Students with higher associate learning skills exhibit high associative responses when they encounter new concepts that could be linked to previously learned concepts. In particular, those students who have higher divergent associative learning skills also have higher possibility of bringing up original and creative ideas, leading to better learning outcomes. Students with higher divergent associative learning skills also have higher classification abilities to abstract higher order concept classes from a set of concepts (for example, abstracting the class "mammals" by looking at a list that contains horse, whale and human).

Students with higher inductive reasoning ability also exhibit higher divergent associative learning skills. A higher inductive reasoning ability allows students to extend their abstraction process to include other previously learnt knowledge and find examples that are not directly linked to the concept currently being learned. Students with higher divergent associative learning skills also infer metaphors much better than other students.

Students with higher divergent associative learning skills exhibit lower ability to filter relevant data for the problem at hand. Since these students exhibit higher capability for divergence, they are less capable of focusing narrowly, which leads to less emphasis on identifying what is relevant and what is not. Similarly, these students also show signs of wider exploration of the learning content rather than following a pre-defined navigation path. However, these students are more prone to looking for overall meaning instead of going down to the details of individual concepts. Adaptivity and personalisation mechanisms can support such students by helping them in narrowing down their focus to more relevant topics in the context of current learning goals while still providing them with sufficient width and depth to suit their cognitive abilities.

Students with higher divergent associative learning skills tend to have higher working memory capacity, compared to those students who have lower divergent associative learning skills. Similarly, students with higher working memory capacity exhibit better associative learning ability compared to those with lower working memory capacity. Higher divergent associative learning skills are also linked with better learning comprehension of students.

Adaptive and personalized learning environments can use various clues from students' actions during the learning process to identify the level of their divergent associative learning skills. For example, a student who is exhibiting a high inductive reasoning ability, who shows low competence in filtering relevant data for the task at hand, or who has a tendency to explore wider learning content instead of focusing on a pre-defined navigational path, is likely to have higher divergent associative learning skills. On the other hand, a student who stays on a linear pre-defined navigational path, who is less capable of classifying higher order concepts, or who has low working memory capacity, is likely to have lower divergent associative learning skills. The more clues support certain levels of divergent associative learning skills, the more reliably an adaptive and personalized learning environment can conclude the level of that student's divergent associative learning skills.

Test your understanding

- What is the main characteristic of divergent associative learning skill?
- What is the relation between working memory capacity and divergent associative learning skill?

Assessing cognitive abilities during learning process

Students with different cognitive abilities learn differently and need different kinds of support during the learning process. It is therefore important for adaptive and personalized learning environments to know individual students' levels of various cognitive abilities. We shall now look at how adaptive and personalized learning environments can measure students' various cognitive abilities when students are going through the learning process. The information about individual students' cognitive abilities is stored in a separate component of the environment, called a cognitive trait model.

A cognitive trait model is only one component of the overall student model that an adaptive and personalized learning environment maintains. The environment also needs to identify students' competence levels in the subject areas (also known as competence model or performance model). In addition, the environment may also have information about students' learning styles, and even physiological data, such as heart rate, temperature, pupil dilation and other characteristics to identify stress levels, attention, and other physical symptoms to optimize learning process. Here we shall focus only on the cognitive trait model.

One of the important characteristics of the cognitive trait model is that it is not dependent on any subject matter. Students' cognitive abilities can be measured and stored in the cognitive trait model by the adaptive and personalized learning environments during any subject matter students are learning. Similarly, the information about the cognitive abilities of a student can be used by the environment any time for providing adaptivity and per-sonalization for any subject matter even if the cognitive abilities were measured when student was learning a different subject. It is also possible that different cognitive abilities stored in the cognitive trait model were measured at different times during learning of completely different subject matters, and they can still be used together or even separately when student is learning something else. For example, the environment may provide adaptivity related to working memory capacity when student is learning a concept in physics and using working memory for some calculations, even when the working memory was calculated when the student was learning a mathematics concept.

Another characteristic of the cognitive trait model that differentiates it from other components of the student model is that it remains valid for long periods of time. A performance model, in contrast, is valid only while a student is learning a particular subject. Once the student has finished learning that particular subject, the only information the performance model can usefully provide is that the student has achieved competence in that subject. This information is not really very useful when the student starts to learn another subject, except perhaps to know whether the student is ready to start another subject if that subject was dependent on the subject the student has already learnt. The cognitive trait model, on the other hand, retains full use when students move from one subject to another. Any new information about students' cognitive abilities that the cognitive trait model has learnt during the learning process of a subject is equally valid and useful when students move to learn another subject.

So, in some aspects, the cognitive trait model is complementary to other components in the student model. At the same time, it is possible to separate the cognitive trait model from other components of the student model and transfer it to other learning environments, instead of creating a whole new cognitive trait model in the new learning environment and trying to measure student's cognitive abilities once again. Since cognitive abilities are not dependent on subject matter and are applicable for long periods of time, as soon as the cognitive trait model is plugged in a new learning environment, the environment's adaptivity and personalization mechanism can start to use the cognitive trait model and provide adaptivity and personalization just like it knows the student for long time.

Reflection

- Why is the cognitive trait model component of the student model not sufficient for providing adaptivity and personalization to the students? What characteristics of the students will be missing if the cognitive trait was the only component in the student model? How would it affect the adaptivity and personalization support?

Structure of cognitive trait model

Figure 4.1 provides an example of the cognitive trait model.

Let us look at how an adaptive and personalized learning environment measures cognitive abilities of a student and stores them in the cognitive trait model. It all starts when a student starts using the environment for learning. All activities that a student undertakes during the learning process happens on the interface of the learning environment. As the student explores the learning

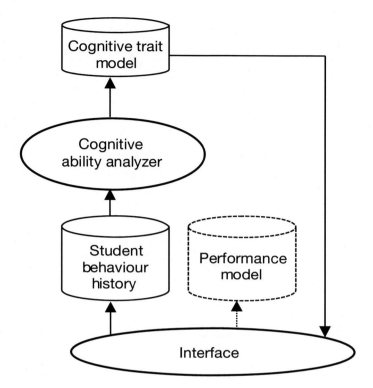

FIGURE 4.1 Example cognitive trait model

content, selects any links, undertakes any quiz, checks out posts in the discussion form, or gets involved in any other learning activity, all his/her actions are captured and sent to the student behaviour history. These actions are also supplied to the performance model, which separately analyzes the student's performance. The data in the student behaviour history is then sent to the cognitive ability analyzer that measures the levels of the student's cognitive abilities and sends them to the cognitive trait model.

The cognitive ability analyzer component is made up of three parts (see Figure 4.2).

When the data from the student behaviour history arrives in the cognitive ability analyzer, it is sent to the activity pattern detector component. This component uses data mining techniques to analyze whether the data shows ant pattern that can give clue of any cognitive ability. For example, the data could show the navigation path a student is taking within the learning content, which

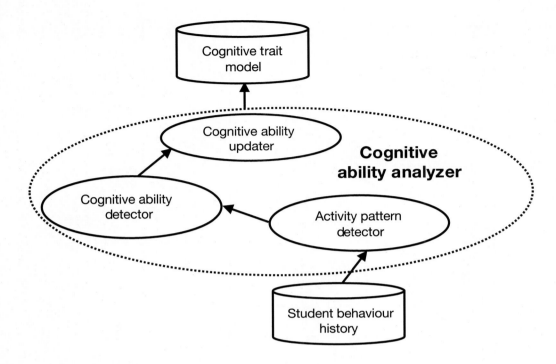

FIGURE 4.2 Cognitive ability analyzer

may give clues about working memory capacity and divergent associative learning skills. Or, the data could reveal that the student has compared two examples and has now moved to the definition of the concept used in both examples. This may give clues to the student's inductive reasoning ability. Once the activity pattern detector identifies a useful pattern, it sends that pattern to the cognitive ability detector component. This component applies a neural network which is trained to identify two things: which of the cognitive abilities can be detected from the activity pattern, and what level of that cognitive ability the student is exhibiting in that activity pattern. For example, if the activity pattern shows that the student is following a strictly linear path in the learning content, it would be one of the clues for low level working memory capacity. It also shows divergent associative learning skill with low level.

The cognitive ability detector component sends its analysis to the cognitive ability updater component. This component keeps receiving the analysis and aggregating it for one session. At the end of the session, when the student leaves the learning environment, the cognitive ability updater analyses the overall situation. For example, within a session, some activity patterns may have indicated low working memory capacity but the majority of the patterns indicated high working memory capacity. The cognitive ability updater aggregates that data and calculates the final level of working memory capacity. So, if there were three patterns indicating low working memory and 10 indicating high working memory, the cognitive ability updater will calculate the final value of working memory ability to be high in that session. It will then store that information in the cognitive trait model as a separate record for that session. The more sessions in the cognitive trait model that indicate a similar level of a particular cognitive ability, the more reliable that analysis becomes and the more confidently the adaptive and personalized learning environment can use that information for providing adaptive and personalized support to the student.

Learning activities

1. Select a topic in a subject of your choice.
2. Create several learning activities for students on that topic.
3. Identify what actions students will do in those activities that could be recorded in the student behaviour history.
4. Identify at least two activity patterns that could be used by cognitive ability analyzer to measure the students' working memory capacity.

Share your ideas with your colleagues and ask them to critique. Provide feedback to your colleagues on their ideas in return.

Links

Learning Theories -> Learning Concepts -> Learning Domains: www.instructionaldesign.org/

Resources

Memory span: https://en.wikipedia.org/wiki/Memory_span
OSPAN—Operation span task: www.cognitiveatlas.org/task/operation_span_task

Web-OSPAN—a web-based tool to measure working memory capacity: http://io.acad.athabascau.ca/~kinshuk/webospan/

References

Baddeley, A. (2000). Working memory. *Encyclopedia of psychology, 8*. Washington, US: American Psychological Association, pp. 276–279.

Baddeley, A. D. (1992). Working memory. *Science, 255*, 556–559.

Lin, T. (2007). Cognitive Trait Model for Adaptive Learning Environments. *PhD Thesis*, Palmerston North, New Zealand: Massey University.

five
Content-Based Adaptivity and Personalization

In computer-based learning environments, the success of the learning process largely depends on how the environments present the domain knowledge to the students, change their presentation in terms of complexity and granularity to suit the students' progress, and consider the characteristics of the devices being used by the students and the preferences of the students. The adaptivity and personalization mechanisms in such environments are expected to seamlessly adapt to the students' environment anytime and anywhere.

Content in such environments is presented to the students through various multimedia objects. Historically, many environments put more emphasis on the affective and psychomotor aspects while using multimedia and tried to lure the students by using spectacular effects provided by images, animations, video and sound (Pham, 1997). In such environments, the emphasis shifted from adequate learning outcomes and cognitive development, and the goal of knowledge acquisition was also diluted.

With recent advances in mobile technologies, and more and more mobile devices being used by the students in the learning process, consideration also

FIGURE 5.1 Page level adaptation

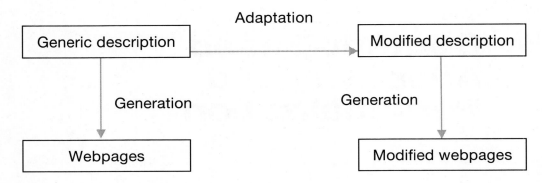

FIGURE 5.2 Conceptual level adaptation

needs to be given to mobile adaptation of content. There are two ways such adaptation can take place: page level adaptation and conceptual level adaptation. The page level adaptation takes an existing webpage that can be displayed by a standard browser on a standard computer display and modifies its HTML code to make it suitable for mobile device (Figure 5.1).

Conceptual level adaptation, on the other hand, starts with a generic abstract description of the content, from which the actual web pages could be generated. Adaptation then takes the abstract description as its input and derives another abstract description for mobile devices. The pages generated out of this modified specification are better suitable for specific mobile clients.

Test your understanding

1. What are the key factors for success of the learning process in computer-based learning environments?
2. What is the difference between page level adaptation and conceptual level adaptation?

Multimedia based content representation

In computer-based learning environments, content is available in various forms, and various multimedia formats are used by the teachers to explain various concepts. It is important to understand the relation between multimedia and the needs of instruction to be able to provide appropriately adapted and personalized learning experience to the individual students. Any effective adaptive and personalized learning environment is expected to change its presentation of domain knowledge according to the students' needs and progress. For example, the environment should present simple content and overview to the students who are new to that particular topic. When students have shown competence in the basic content, then it should increase the complexity and go in detail. So, a good learning environment should provide content differently to new students and to the students who have already learnt something.

So, how do we create computer-based learning environments that can provide content effectively? For this, we need to have some sort of educational framework that could guide the creation of effective and efficient tutoring strategies for a given domain that can be used by the adaptivity and personalization mechanism to take autonomous decisions regarding content presentation. It is important to remember that computer-based learning environments can be used by the students any time. It is therefore possible that the students will use the environment when no teacher or subject expert is present. That means, if the environment is supposed to change its presentation of the content for different students, it needs to have some rules for that purpose. The environment needs to know what to do when a new student comes, and what to do when a student who already has some competency in that content wants to learn further. The environment needs to have appropriate tutoring strategies or rules by which it can change the presentation itself, without requiring a human teacher to do it manually. This is no different from different pedagogies used by the teachers to teach different content in physical classrooms and different learning tasks given to the students for different purposes.

There are several educational frameworks available in the literature outlining various tutoring strategies for specific learning tasks. These frameworks make sure that the presentation of concepts on the learning environment's interface is meaningful and effective for learning. Any good learning environment needs to understand both the students and the domain. It needs to consider the students' needs and then apply appropriate learning theories for that particular domain and learning task. A nice looking presentation, rich with multimedia, on its own does not guarantee learning. There are so many types of rich multimedia objects at the disposal of learning environment developers nowadays, for example, educational games, animations, videos, virtual reality and simulations, that it is tempting to use them to make fancy looking attractive interfaces. While it is certainly important that the content is appealing to the students, the application of learning theories ensures that various components of the content are presented to the students in such a way that effective and efficient learning takes place. Adaptivity and personalization mechanisms in the learning environments can combine the information available about the student, the information about the domain, and the rules elicited from learning theories to customize the presentation of content to the individual students.

It is important to remember that the only component of the learning environment that the students see is the interface. If the environment contains lots of good functionality, but it is not reflected on the interface, then all that functionality has no use. For the students, it is like that functionality does not even exist. So, the interface has to be developed very carefully.

Designing adaptive and personalized learning environments

We shall now look at designing adaptive and personalized learning environments where the presentation of various types of multimedia content on the learning environment's interface is guided by a suitable educational framework. This approach enables the presentation of multimedia objects (such as audio, images, animations, simulations and so on) into a multimedia interface world where the relationships of the objects to the world are governed by the tutoring strategies provided by the educational framework.

The students need to be provided with various forms of interactivity depending on the pedagogical goal of the learning at a particular moment. For this purpose, we first need to identify the usefulness of various multimedia objects with respect to various learning tasks. Not every multimedia object is good for every learning task. Once a learning activity is selected by the learning system for a particular student, the adaptivity and personalization mechanism then needs to consider the best suited multimedia objects to represent that activity.

The guidelines provided under this approach are not general interface design guidelines. These guidelines are specific pedagogy-based guidelines for learning environment interfaces using an educational framework. These guidelines are complementary to the generally accepted interface design guidelines in human-computer interaction field and are aimed to assist the designers of learning environments from the students' point-of-view—what do students need in a particular educational context?

Application of guidelines

Since these guidelines work within an educational framework, let us take an example. We shall discuss these guidelines for domain competence in task oriented disciplines, such as engineering and medicine. The first task in selecting a suitable educational framework for such disciplines is to identify the learning goal and then select an educational framework that supports that learning goal. These type of disciplines require hands-on activities that are primarily based on decision making skills. In these disciplines, both cognitive and physical skills are very important. Therefore, we shall apply cognitive apprenticeship framework which supports mastery of both cognitive and physical skills during the learning process, and has been found very effective for task-oriented disciplines.

The cognitive apprenticeship framework was first suggested by Allan Collins, John Seely Brown and Susan E. Newman. It divides the learning process into three stages. In the first stage, the students study expert's task solving patterns to develop their own cognitive models about the tasks, tools and solutions of the domain. This stage is called *Modelling*. In the second stage, the students solve tasks by consulting a tutorial component. This stage is called *Coaching*. In the final stage, students gain mastery by repeated practice, and the tutorial activity is gradually reduced with the students' improving performance. This stage is termed as *Fading*. More details of the cognitive apprenticeship framework can be found in Collins, Brown and Newman (1989).

Let us analyze the usefulness of various multimedia objects for different stages of the cognitive apprenticeship framework. At first, when students start to learn a topic, they have no competency in either the knowledge or skills of that topic. At that stage, students need to passively observe how the experts do certain tasks in order to obtain direct instruction for knowledge. This can be facilitated by providing text, images, pictures, animations, videos, audios, and other multimedia objects that allow for passive observation. Once the students have acquired some basic knowledge but still no skills, direct instruction for skills with few exploration possibilities can be provided by some active observation through those multimedia objects that require some action for gaining deeper knowledge, such as image maps, textual links, interactive videos, pictorial virtual reality and so on. These multimedia objects do not actually provide any subject related skills, but they require students' active participation to seek more details.

After the observation (modelling) stage, the students need to move to the coaching stage where they will engage in simple problem solving tasks and get feedback on their performance. This can be achieved by simple actions and decisions requiring multimedia objects. For example, pictorial virtual reality can be used to ask the correct position of a part in a structure, or a flow-chart can be used to ask a decision point. This would then lead to advance exploration possibilities, where more complex action and decision oriented multimedia objects, such as simulations and flowcharts can be highly useful. These objects require students to use their cognitive abilities. Based on the students' performance, the adaptivity and personalization mechanism can provide appropriate feedback to the students. Depending on the nature of the problem-solving task, such feedback can be provided through a variety of multi-media objects, ranging from text, images and audio to all the way through videos and interactive videos.

As students start to gain mastery, the fading starts, and the assessment of the mastery can be obtained by evaluation and delayed feedback, once again through a variety of multimedia objects. Further practice can be provided by more complex scenarios, using simulations and flowcharts for different scenarios, and transfer from generic knowledge to real-life scenarios can then be facilitated through various authoring tools and the tools of the trade using various multimedia objects. Even co-operation and teamwork skills, that are very relevant in the work context, can be facilitated through authoring and communication tools using various multimedia objects.

Learning activities

1. Select a topic in a science subject.
2. For each stage of the cognitive apprentice framework, create an activity.
3. Select an example multimedia object for that activity. Explain why that object is suitable for that activity.

Guidelines for selection of multimedia objects

Let us now look at various guidelines for a selection of multimedia objects. They can be divided into three categories: selection of multimedia objects for representing content, selection of multimedia objects to facilitate navigation, and integration of multimedia objects.

Selection of multimedia objects for representing content

The first guideline relates to the suitability of the multimedia object for a particular task. Multimedia objects have specific characteristics that make them suitable for different tasks. For example, audio is good for stimulating imagination. In childhood, parents and grandparents used to tell stories to their children and grandchildren, something like "Once upon a time, there was a prince in far, far away kingdom. He lived in a grand palace . . ." Such stories were not only entertaining but also a great medium for stimulating imagination in children. Children can start to visualize in their mind the scenario described through the audio. Video, on the other hand, is suitable for showing action. It is good to demonstrate a process or step by step procedure of a task. However, video suffers from the fact that it may fail to highlight certain useful learning concepts if there are other more attention-catching activities going on simultaneously. For example, in a video of a medical operating room, in which students are watching a surgery procedure, students may focus on a sudden blood spill instead of the actions of the surgeons and nurses that are important from a learning point-of-view. Text on the other hand is good to convey details. So, if someone is watching a video, a text message can be given to highlight certain information, something like, "look at this video and take special note of the action starting at 17 seconds. There you will see that a nurse is preparing equipment . . .". Similarly, diagrams are suitable for conveying ideas. They can be used even when the thoughts are not very clear. Diagrams include outlines and sketches, which are powerful tools to convey even vague ideas. One can simply draw some sketches to bring various ideas together, and the process can help those ideas to emerge into clear concepts.

The level of a student's domain competence also influences the selection of multimedia objects for representing content. For this purpose, a curriculum should follow a granular structure to allow assessment of individual units. This will enable the adaptivity and personalization mechanism to make context based selections of multimedia objects to suit individual student's needs. The granularity of the domain content needs consideration in two dimensions: first, the advancement in curriculum, e.g., initially an abstract concept by using animation of a concrete instantiation of the concept, followed by more complex abstract representation; and, second, details of the content, e.g., simple observation by static diagrams at novice level, and active observation using virtual reality with full complexity at advanced level.

Another guideline for the selection of multimedia objects relates to expectations. When students are learning some content, they have certain expectations about what kind of multimedia representation they need for the current learning task. Similarly, there are certain domain-specific constraints and expectations about what kind of representation is needed. So, if the expectations of the students and that of a domain do not match, then the best strategy is to provide presentations in more than one form to suit all expectations. For example, it is possible that a student has a preference for visual content while a domain requires some explanations which need representation in a textual format. In that case, it is better to provide both.

References to already learned material and accessing it again when learning a similar new concept is an important task in the learning process. Such revisiting enables students to link newly learned content to previous learned content in order to make connections between different knowledge components and understand the concepts in different contexts. Therefore, the adaptivity and personalization mechanism should enable students to revisit previously learned content as and when a new concept of a similar kind needs to be learned by the students. Moreover, the new content should be provided to the students using similar multimedia objects as the previously learned concept to reduce the cognitive overload on the students.

It is important to use as many senses in the learning process, such as visual, aural and tactile senses, as possible so that the students can fully engage in the learning process and do not get distracted due to the unused sensory channels. For example, when students are learning, there may be other activities going on in the background, for example, if a television is on and if a student is only using, say his/her eyes to observe the learning content, then the sound from the television may distract the student from learning. However, if a student is also listening to the content explanations using headphones while observing visual content, then the chances of distraction are significantly reduced. So, the reception of learning enhances if the representation of domain content involves various sensory channels.

If there are multiple multimedia objects available in the learning environment to represent the same task/concept, then the adaptivity and personalization mechanism should select those multimedia objects which best suit the current context. For example, if there is a simulation available for a concept and the same concept is also explained in text, then the system should possibly allow a novice student to interact with the simulation for detailed understanding. Once the student has explored various aspects of simulation and has acquired the basic knowledge and skills, the textual object can be made available for review purposes and to ensure that the student did not miss any important information. Demands of the domain should determine which multimedia objects should be used for which task and in which context.

Sometime it is important to provide simplistic scenarios in the learning process, particularly for novice students so that they do not get lost in complex details. However, in such cases, it is important to let the students know that the current representation is a simplified version of the actual real-life scenario, so that they do not get the wrong impression. For example, appropriate messages should be given while showing schematic diagrams and animations of the processes that do not show the real objects.

Selection of multimedia objects to facilitate navigation

Multimedia objects are also used in the learning environments for providing navigation links between different learning content. It is important to use multimedia objects for such linking in a way that the students have clear understanding of what will happen when they click on that navigation object. The adaptivity and personalization mechanism should also make sure that students' expectations of the outcome while activating a navigation link object are matched with the presentation of actual resulting interface connected to the link. For example, if a student clicks on a word while reading some text, then linking that word to a quiz on that word would probably not match with the student's expectations.

The type of multimedia object used for linking should suit the context and the student's expectations of the outcome of the navigation. The objects should be selected in a way that they match the task and the use of the object should not be confusing for the student. In other words, the object should not put an additional cognitive load on the student. The use of the object should also not deviate the student's attention from the main task of learning. In fact, the use of object should be so intuitive for the task it has been selected for that the object should not stand out. Navigation links themselves do not provide learning. They are there to simply move the student from one part of the learning environment to another. So, if the object used for the navigation itself is very complex or unusual, then it will unnecessarily distract the student's attention from learning tasks.

The navigation objects can be classified into two broad categories: interaction objects and interactive objects (Bodart & Vanderdonckt, 1994). Interaction objects provide transition from one part of the environment to another on the student's explicit initiative. Examples include push buttons, radio buttons and check boxes. These objects are typically not part of the content. The use of these objects require students to think about navigation explicitly outside of the learning context. Interactive objects, on the other hand, facilitate a contextual transfer recommended by the system. For example, if a student is reading some content and there is a word with a link, then the student can click on it to get more details. These transfers happen naturally within the learning process and do not require students to think about them explicitly outside of the learning context. Since these transfers typically take place from the content itself, interactive objects are also generally the content object themselves, such as links in texts and clickable images (image maps).

Let us look at different tasks in computer-based learning environments where navigation objects are used:

- Direct succession from one learning unit to another in knowledge hierarchy: such transfers arise from the current context, such as a link in the text or a message after completing a learning unit. These transfers therefore require interactive objects. For example, after learning Newton's first law of motion, direct succession would lead to Newton's second law of motion.

- Succession to an analogous learning unit for comparative learning or to a unit related to another aspect of the content currently being learnt: These transfers are explicit and therefore require the use of interaction objects. For example, after learning from an example of Archimedes' principle, this kind of transfer would lead to another example of Archimedes' principle.

- Succession to the finer details of certain content once some missing or misconceptions are identified: These transfers are very contextual and it is necessary to maintain the context during transfer. Therefore, interactive objects, such as image maps, can be used.

- Definitions: When students need to see definitions of some terms, these need to be provided without losing the current context. For that, pop-up windows can be used which can be shown to the student. Such definitions should be available only for the duration the student is interested in them and is requesting them explicitly (such as by pressing the mouse button). These links provide a referential summary of the terms, and hence should be initiated from the terms themselves.

- Excursions: While learning a concept, students sometime need to do excursions to other units in the learning environment to access additional information for better understanding of the current concept. Navigation to such learning units outside the current knowledge hierarchy requires a way back to the current learning unit without losing the current context. The adaptivity and personalization mechanism needs to ensure that the context for such excursions is broad enough to cover the essence of the current unit and the multimedia objects used for such excursions are easily and distinctively recognised as having a two-way navigation possibility.

- Assessment: Succession to assessment activities in the learning environments requires careful consideration. Such transfers should result from the environment's inference of learning criteria fulfilment by the student for a particular learning unit, and the adaptivity and personalization mechanism should select the assessment task within the context of the current learning unit. The multimedia objects used for such navigation should make it clear to the student that interacting with those objects will lead to assessment. They should also make it clear whether such assessment is for informal self-learning or for formal assessment.

Test your understanding

1. Please identify for which kind of learning task each of these objects are suitable:

   a. audio
   b. simulation
   c. text

2. Please identify appropriate multimedia objects for each of the following transfers:

   a. textual links from the content
   b. textual links from messages
   c. clickable parts in images

Integration of multimedia objects for content representation:

The final set of guidelines relates to the integration of various multimedia objects on the learning environment interface. An adaptive and personalized learning environment needs to consider the requirements of the students and the domain, as well as the impact of the multimedia objects themselves while deciding on which multimedia objects should be presented to the students for certain learning content at any given point in time.

There should not be more than one active multimedia object using the same sensory channel at a time on the interface. For example, if there are two videos presented to a student at the same time, it would be difficult if not impossible for the student to observe each video properly. The videos will interfere with each other by grabbing the student's attention at the same time. The only exception is the comparative analysis of two activities, where students should look at both activities at the same time to be able to compare and spot any differences.

Integration of multimedia objects should be complementary and synchronised. For example, when a student is watching a video about how plants grow from seed, a complementary audio highlighting various changes in the plant's structure would be very useful. However, it is important that the same learning content is not repeated using different multimedia objects at the same time. For example, if there is a piece of text that the students need to read, an audio object reading that text at the same time when the student is also trying to read would interfere with the student's reading activity, and may be even more problematic if the speed of reading in the audio does not match the student's own pace of reading. However, it is quite fine to have audio prompts giving short advice on what parts of text require more careful attention, for example, due to higher complexity of that part. Such prompts will be complementary to the student's reading activity.

Integration of decision intensive multimedia objects is not recommended due to their high cognitive load demands. For example, more than one simulation object on the same interface will likely result in high cognitive overload and may impair the learning activity.

If there are different types of multimedia objects that have a similar initial appearance, they should not be put together on the interface to avoid confusion. For example, if there is a simulation object and a virtual reality object, and both look similar in appearance, then it is not recommended to put them on the same learning environment interface at the same time.

Integration of dynamic and static observation objects should be such that both objects should not use the same sensory channel at the same time. For example, if the content requires a student to observe an image and a video to learn the concept effectively, then the learning environment should make it very clear to the student that the image will not disappear in a short time and will be available after the student has watched the video. That way, the student will not be forced to use the same sensory channel for two multimedia objects at the same time.

Reflection

Analyze these multimedia object pairs and identify whether they can be used together at the same time on the learning environment interface or not:

Text and audio
Image and simulation
Audio and animation

Test your understanding

1. Why is it important to engage as many sensory channels of the students as possible during the learning process?
2. Why is it important to refer to previously learned material if the concept currently being learnt is similar in nature to the previously learned concept?
3. What is the difference between interaction objects and interactive objects?
4. Give examples of the navigation objects that should be used for succession to an analogous learning unit.
5. What precautions should the learning environment designers take while selecting multimedia objects for transfer to assessment?

A representative scenario

Let us apply the guidelines we discussed in this chapter in a practical scenario of medical education, with a particular focus on students learning the structure and functionality of ear and related diseases. Since these guidelines work within a particular educational framework, we shall apply the cognitive apprenticeship framework as it covers both theoretical knowledge and cognitive skills. Table 5.1 shows various stages of learning for this scenario.

The first set of guidelines look at selecting multimedia objects to represent the content. Depending on the current competence level of the individual students, the adaptivity and personalization mechanism would start the learning process for a new student with a passive observation using the structure and

TABLE 5.1 Various stages of learning the structure and functionality of ear and related diseases

Stage of learning	Tasks
Student new to the topic: primary focus on instruction	• Passive and active observation of structure and functionality of ear • Observation of basic rules of physics that explain how sounds travels
More focused learning after identifying misconceptions and missing conceptions	• Exploring structure and functionality of ear • Understanding of various rules of physics related to the sound travel • Passive and active observation of diseases related to ear
Development of cognitive skills after acquiring basic understanding	• Exploring the diseases of ear and associated diagnosis • Interpreting various medical graphs and instrument readings related to ear diseases
Applying the skills and knowledge	• Undertaking specific problem scenarios to practice treating the diseases of ear • Gaining mastery by repetitive practice of large number of variety of cases of ear diseases

functionality of the ear using text and typical images. Active observations then follow using pictures with clickable parts to zoom into finer details. Animations are then used to provide advanced observations. Three types of animations can be used: automatic animations that the students simply observe; user controlled animations that the students can stop, go backward and go forward; and, user initiated animations that the students can start as and when the student is ready to use. Following the observation phase, simulations are used by the students for acquiring cognitive skills. More realistic scenarios are provided by using virtual reality objects. Even more realistic cases are provided by videos of actual cases. Decision making skills are provided to the students by flowcharts.

A number of navigation object selection techniques are used following the second set of guidelines for providing navigational links between different learning content. For example, the adaptivity and personalization mechanism can use the hyperlinks to individual malleus, incus and stapes bones within the text that explains the overall structure of the ear. The image of the overall structure of the ear can also be used for navigation to those components of the ear that are found to be of importance for the individual students.

Various guidelines for integration of multimedia objects can also be used by the adaptivity and personalization mechanism. For example, the concept of "appropriate sound energy routing" can be presented by two comparative animations, one using a rock as the medium for sound travel and another using metal. The structure of the bones can be presented as an image with alternative text and as a virtual reality object to prevent confusion due to similar initial visual states.

One approach for the application of these guidelines is to implement them as a filter between the student and the content, governed by the adaptivity and personalization mechanism, supported by the student model (the component of the learning environment that collects and stores the information about the individual students). Figure 5.3 shows a schematic diagram of such an implementation.

Once the adaptivity and personalization mechanism of the learning environment has identified the content to be presented to the student, based on student characteristics, pedagogical requirements and the needs of the domain, a "content validator" component validates each multimedia object for compliance with the guidelines. If the content is successfully validated, it is passed on to the "content renderer" component that shows the content on

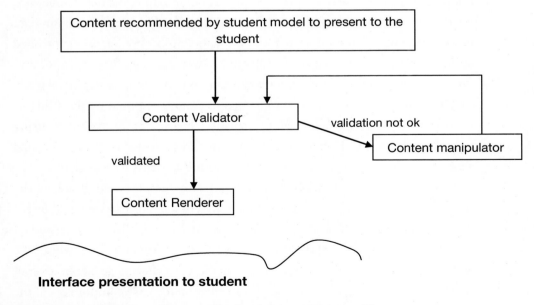

Interface presentation to student

FIGURE 5.3 Adaptivity and personalization implemented as a filter

the student's screen. If the "content validator" identifies any violation of the guidelines, it sends the content to the "content manipulator" component. The "content manipulator" attempts to refine the content selection and identifies alternative objects, if available, based on priorities set through the student characteristics, pedagogical constraints and the requirements of the domain. The refined content is then sent again to the "content validator", which if the content can now be validated, sends it to the "content renderer". If the content still violates the guidelines, it is sent back to the "content manipulator" for further refinement and the cycle continues.

References

Bodart F. & Vanderdonckt J. (1994). Visual layout techniques in multimedia applications. Conference Companion, CHI'94, Boston, Mass., 121–122.

Collins A., Brown J. S. & Newman S. E. (1989). Cognitive Apprenticeship: Teaching the crafts of reading, writing and mathematics. Knowing, Learning and Instruction (Ed. L. B. Resnick), Hillsdale, NJ: Lawrence Erlbaum Associates, 453–494.

Pham B. (1997). Development of educational multimedia systems. Australasian Association for Engineering Education—9th Annual Convention and Conference, Dec. 14–17, 1997, Ballarat, Australia.

six
Adaptivity and Personalization in Exploration-Based Learning

Students in online learning environments are expected to explore various learning contents and engage in various learning activities on their own to acquire knowledge and skills. Various factors affect the adaptivity and personalization of learning in such exploration-based scenarios. We shall look at various components of exploration-based learning, and how students can be supported through adaptivity and personalization in the learning process in such environments. We shall also look at designing adaptive and personalized learning environments for exploratory learning.

All student-centered activities are primarily exploration activities. These activities are critical in the learning process as they enable students to find various pieces of information from various sources and integrate them in a meaningful manner to create knowledge. Pedagogically, such learning is termed as "constructivist learning", based on the theory of constructivism by Jean Piaget (1967). Exploration activities are typically self-initiated and are highly dependent on the student's goals, motivation and learning needs. Learning by exploration is a particularly effective technique for task-oriented disciplines, such as engineering, computer science and medicine. In learning by exploration, students explore different information items at different places, conduct various learning activities, including hands-on activities, and then integrate those with previously learned knowledge. That integration process creates knowledge. Exploration-based learning therefore provides not only the skills of the domain but also the understanding of the embedded concepts.

Various types of learning environments have been developed over the years based on learning by exploration. These include hypermedia systems, simulation systems and others that provide students with exploration environments where students can explore various paths to solve problems. For example, in hypermedia systems, students can click different links. When students do not understand some concept or some term, and if that term has a link, the students can click on that link to go to the page that explains that term. In simulation systems, on the other hand, the students can change various parameters and values of the parameters to observe the effects.

Learning in exploration-based learning environments happens by accessing various types of multimedia objects, such as hypertext, images, video, audio, animations, simulations, and so on. Students search these relevant multimedia objects during the exploration process to comprehend the information and to acquire domain concepts and skills. Comprehension and acquisition involve mutually integrating the information from different resources, and integrating new information into existing knowledge.

The exploration process in the exploration-based learning environments requires two components: multimedia objects that provide information, and various actions that students need to do on those multimedia objects as part of exploration (Kinshuk, Lin and Patel, 2006). Students can search various multimedia objects, select certain parameters, apply intermediate results, and integrate multiple multimedia objects. All these actions are part of exploration. The combination of multimedia objects and associated actions is termed as "exploration space" within which students move and learn (Kashihara et al., 1997). Actions are a very important component of exploration-based learning. For example, let us assume that if there is a webpage that contains information for the students to learn, and that the webpage contains some static text and images, and nothing else. The only activities students can do on such a webpage are to read the text and look at the images. Since there are no actual actions to be performed by the students, it will be difficult to justify that such a webpage provides opportunities for exploration. On the other hand, if there were some hyperlinks on the webpage for students to click on to find more information, if there were simulations where students could change some parameters, if there were some image maps for students to click on certain parts of the image to get further details, then all those kinds of actions would have contributed towards exploration.

Exploration-based learning, by its nature, requires the students to freely explore various parts of the learning content, so that they are able to integrate various types of information to construct knowledge. Obviously, if the students are not able to explore properly, learning by exploration cannot happen. However, unrestricted exploration also has problems that need to be considered. For example, if students do not know what to explore and how to explore, then the learning process will be hindered. This is particularly true for those students who have not yet mastered the meta-learning skills of how to effectively search appropriate information, how to identify what information is relevant and what is not, and how to integrate different information pieces that are relevant, in order to construct meaningful new knowledge. When such students attempt to learn through the exploration-based learning approach in a large information space, they may find it difficult to select the information pieces that are right for them at that moment, with respect to the topic they are learning and the level of competence they currently have. This may require students to exert excessive mental efforts in the learning process which may cause cognitive overload. Many of us can relate to this in our own experiences of searching information on the Internet, where the search engine returned thousands of search results and we felt overwhelmed in trying to find those results that are useful to our purpose. Most of us do not go past the first few search results pages, even when we know that there may be some useful results in later pages.

If the exploration space is quite wide, there is also the risk of students getting lost in too much information. This is similar to getting "lost in hyperspace", where people browsing information on the Internet lose their focus of what they wanted to look for and get disoriented due to the sheer amount of information available. It is important to understand that people getting lost in hyperspace do not experience it because they are not hard working or are disinterested in the task. In fact, it is unlikely for those people who are not hard working or are disinterested in the task to get lost in hyperspace since they are unlikely to go deep in their search efforts anyway. When the students are learning in a wide exploration space, they have certain learning goals. However, at the same time, they may also have many personal interests. When they start to explore the space with the aim to find relevant information for their current learning goals, it is likely that they will also find information that is not directly relevant to their current learning goals but is related to one of their personal interests. At that point, if the students do not remain focused and start to explore the information that is related to their personal interests, they will move away from their current learning goals. It does not mean that they will not learn anything. They will certainly learn but that learning will not benefit the current learning goals.

For example, if a student of a history subject is searching for information on the ship Titanic while exploring the learning content, he/she may also find content related to the movie with the same name. If that student is interested in movies, it is possible that he/she may start to explore the content related to the movie instead of the content related to the historical ship. The wider the exploration space is, the more the learning content is available, and the more there are chances that the student will find content related to his/her personal interests alongside the content related to the current learning goal. In that situation, a student who has good meta-learning skills would probably book-mark the content related to personal interest for later use and continue with the current learning goal. However, for a novice student, the chances of getting distracted from the current learning goal are high in such a situation.

So, in cases where either students do not yet possess the meta-learning skills needed for what to explore and how to explore, or they may have encountered problems of cognitive overload due to large exploration space, the adaptive and personalized learning environments can customize the selection of exploration techniques that are appropriate in terms of extent and amount of complexity for the individual student, and personalize the exploration space to suit the individual student's current level of competence and his/her current capacity to cope with the cognitive load required for the exploration activities.

For example, the adaptivity and personalization mechanism can customize the navigation techniques used for exploring the learning content and recommend which exploration techniques would be more appropriate, based on the student's familiarity with the techniques and inherent complexity of those techniques. It can also analyze the available learning content and tailor the information that is presented to the student. It can analyze what kind of learning content is available, which multimedia objects are at appropriate complexity and granularity for the student, and what kinds of actions on those objects the student would find within his/her competency and familiarity zone. Various parameters can be restricted in simulation objects to make it easier for a novice student to interpret the results. The problems can be sequenced in such a way that they focus a student's attention on specific parts of the domain. This would allow for students to have an easier understanding of the domain in a gradual manner. Overall, the purpose of such adaptivity and personalization is to make it easier for the students to search and comprehend domain concepts and knowledge. For this purpose, the adaptivity and personalization mechanism will limit the exploration space for novice students based on the domain complexity and the individual student's competence, understanding level, experience and other personal attributes, and will remove the restrictions gradually as the student progresses in the learning process.

Since the purpose of exploration-based learning is to enable students to learn by exploring content from various sources, limiting exploration space negates the whole purpose of this type of learning. Therefore, it is important for the adaptivity and personalization mechanism to limit the exploration space to a minimum, just to ensure that the cognitive load exerted by the space is within the student's cognitive capability, and to remove those limitations as soon as the student is ready to handle a larger exploration space. For the students with a higher learning competence, the mechanism needs to focus on reducing cognitive load as less as possible. These students typically like the challenges and if the cognitive load is too little, they would get bored and may lose interest in the learning process. On the other hand, students with lower learning competence will require reduction in the cognitive load as much as possible, since these students typically get frustrated when the cognitive load is higher than what they can handle.

Various methods to limit cognitive load

The adaptivity and personalization mechanism can use various methods to limit the cognitive load of students in exploration-based learning. For example, novice students are provided with learning content gradually through scaffolding.

Initially, only the most necessary information is provided and students are guided through the exploration of that information. Once the students start to demonstrate some competency, further multimedia objects with more advanced learning content are gradually added.

The number of total multimedia objects to be presented to the student is decided by the adaptivity and personalization mechanism based on the competency level of the individual student. Once the total number of multimedia objects has been established, the mechanism then decides about the various types of multimedia objects that should be included, so that the student is able to explore the learning content related to his/her current goals adequately without any cognitive overload. For example, if a student has demonstrated better affinity to textual content instead of audio, the mechanism will select the multimedia objects accordingly, as long as the selection aligns with the demands of the domain.

Another aspect is the number of various navigation paths that are available for exploration for the current learning content. For a student who has low short-term memory and cannot handle too much information at a time, if the learning environment provides him/her with all sorts of information related to the current learning goal including all background information, then the student may get overwhelmed and may lose focus. So, for such students, who cannot handle too much information at a time, the adaptivity and personalization mechanism will limit the number of navigation paths and recommend only those paths that are extremely necessary for learning basic knowledge about that concept. For example, if a student with low short term memory is learning about atomic structure in chemistry, then the adaptivity and personalization mechanism will only provide links to the basic knowledge about the atomic structure, such as the components of the atom and their properties. However, if the student has high short-term memory and can handle large amounts of information without losing focus, then the mechanism can also provide background and related information such as the periodic table, how molecules are made of atoms, what valences are, and so on.

Another issue in exploration-based learning is the amount of information to be provided to the student. Once the type and number of multimedia objects have been determined, the next customization for the students in exploration-based learning is about how much information each of those objects should contain. For example, based on various student attributes and the nature of the domain, if the adaptivity and personalization mechanism identifies that the student should be given one simulation and one piece of text, then the mechanism needs to determine how much information should be provided in that simulation and in the text piece. In other words, should the simulation have few parameters for the student to explore or lots of parameters? How long should the text piece be and at what level of complexity? The mechanism also needs to adapt the content of information to each student. For example, which parameters should be given to a particular student in a particular simulation? If a text piece is to be provided, should it contain an overview or some specific details of the concept?

Once the multimedia objects have been selected, the next step is to identify what actions the students can take on those multimedia objects. To support exploration based learning, it is critical that the students are able to take various actions on different multimedia objects. At the same time, those actions should match with individual student's characteristics and competencies. Let us look at some of the example technologies that can be used to enable students to take various actions on the multimedia objects. Various scaffolding techniques can be used to open up learning content gradually to the students as they progress in the learning process and demonstrate competency at every step. For example, the Center for Advanced Research on Language Acquisition (CARLA) provides a comprehensive list of scaffolding techniques for content-based instruction (CARLA, 2015). These include verbal scaffolding techniques focused on language development, procedural scaffolding techniques that include grouping techniques and activity structures and frames, and instructional scaffolding techniques that include tools to support learning. For limiting the number of multimedia objects and the paths available for exploration, various navigation techniques can be used. For example, the adaptivity and personalization mechanism can recommend certain content and highlight those links that are central to the current learning goal. It can also hide less critical paths. The content can be re-ordered so that the student can clearly see the content in the order of importance. Various annotations can be provided to explain the importance of certain content and links. Information tailoring techniques, based on the profile of the student, can be employed to customize the amount of information presented to the student at a given time. Similar customization is also possible for simulations.

Designing adaptive and personalized learning environments for exploration-based learning

The first step in designing adaptive and personalized learning environments is to identify the learning goals of the individual students. As we discussed earlier, students may have many personal interests that may be different from their current learning goals. To be able to keep the students focused on their learning goals and not get distracted by the information which may be personally interesting for them but does not contribute to their current learning goals, the learning environment needs to have up-to-date information about the individual student's learning goals.

The next step is to select various types of multimedia objects that would contribute to various learning goals. Examples of such multimedia objects include hypertext, images, audio, video, animations, simulations, etc. The adaptivity and personalization mechanism needs to be capable of determining what kinds of multimedia objects will be suitable for each learning goal. For each kind of multimedia object, the mechanism should be able to decide what information should be presented through each multimedia object, including the amount of information and the content. For example, which object can provide theoretical concepts and which is more suitable for practical examples, which one can provide a summary of the topic and which is better suited for detailed explanations? The next step is to determine what actions can be done on each of the multimedia objects. For example, in text paragraphs, students can trace the path they took by following links in various pages, and in simulations, students can select various parameters and interpret the results.

Finally, the learning environment needs to be able to customize the learning experience for individual students by applying appropriate restrictions, so that the complexity and amount of learning content presented to the students aligns with their cognitive load. It should neither be too low nor too high. For the novice students, the environment should restrict the exploration space as much as possible, so that the cognitive load does not go beyond what these students can handle. On the other hand, for advance students, the environment should ensure that the learning content is challenging enough so that the students do not get bored.

The restrictions also need to be enforced on various actions that the students take on various multimedia objects used to represent learning content as well as for navigation. An example of the multimedia objects used to represent the learning content is simulation, where the action of selecting various simulation parameters can be restricted to few parameters for a novice student. Similarly, the integration of various multimedia objects can be restricted to those that the student is familiar with, and then unfamiliar objects can be introduced gradually. For the multimedia objects used for navigation, action of tracing links in the text can be customized to only critical ones for the novice students. Similarly, the action of applying intermediate results can be broken into multiple steps so that the cognitive load required for each step does not exceed the limits of the student's cognitive capacity.

Exercise

a. Select one of the following topics:

- conduction mode of heat transfer (physics, see http://en.wikipedia.org/wiki/Heat_transfer for details)
- acids and bases (chemistry, see http://en.wikipedia.org/wiki/Chemistry#Acidity_and_basicity for details)
- Pythagoras's theorem (mathematics, see http://en.wikipedia.org/wiki/Pythagorean_theorem for details)

b. Select at least three types of multimedia objects that would be suitable to represent the learning content of the topic you have selected.

c. Identify what different actions students can take on each of those multimedia objects to explore them.

d. For a novice student, which of those actions will be appropriate and which ones will not be?

Applying restrictions on actions

Determining the level of restriction to apply for the individual student requires consideration of both the characteristics of the domain and the characteristics of the student (also known as the student profile or the student model). Let us look at these two types of characteristics before analyzing what restrictions are influenced by them.

Domain characteristics

The characteristics of the domain that affect the application of restrictions include the type of knowledge (such as know-how and know-why), how detailed the learning content is, and whether the learning content is aimed to provide explanations of a topic (typically suitable for first time learning of a concept) or summary version (generally suited for revisions).

Student characteristics

The characteristics of the students include behavioral attributes (such as preferences and familiarity with the learning process), performance attributes (such as competence in the current topic and in a related domain), cognitive attributes (such as the level of working memory capacity, associative learning skills, and so on), and physiological attributes (such as stress level, alertness, level of tiredness, and so on).

While behavioral, performance and physiological attributes affect learning process, cognitive attributes directly affect the cognitive load that a student can take, and therefore have a major influence on the design of exploration-based learning environments. In the design of such environments, various cognitive attributes of the individual student are mapped to various levels of restrictions and on the actions the student can take on various multimedia objects. We shall first look at the examples of various cognitive attributes and then analyze their effect on the restrictions. Here are some examples:

- *Working memory capacity*, also known as short term memory, enables people to keep a limited amount of information active in the brain for short period of time. George Miller in 1956 suggested the amount of that capacity to be 7±2 chunks of information, although Nelson Cowen in 2000 put forward some cautionary reconsideration of this number.
- *Inductive reasoning ability* is the ability to construct concepts from examples. If the learning content presents many examples based on a certain concept, the students with high inductive reasoning ability would be able to recognize in a very short time the underlying concept by analyzing those examples.

- *Associative learning skill* is the skill to link new knowledge to existing knowledge. Students with high associative learning skills are able to recognize the patterns when they see a new concept that has a similarity with a previously learned concept.
- *Information processing speed* determines how fast a student can acquire information correctly.

Let us further analyze the working memory capacity as an example. Some students can keep 7–2 chunks of information (means 5 chunks) at a time in their brain, whereas others can keep up to 7+2 chunks (so, up to 9 chunks), which is almost double the amount. Therefore, if the learning content requires lots of information to be explored simultaneously, then the students with a lower working memory capacity will find it difficult to cope with that learning content, compared to those students who have a higher working memory capacity.

The adaptivity and personalization mechanism needs to consider this difference while determining what learning content to present to the students. For example, for a student with a low working memory capacity, the number of exploration paths should be reduced to protect the student from getting lost in too much information and from overloading the working memory with vast non-linear structure of the whole exploration space. Such students should be given only those exploration possibilities that are directly relevant to the learning goals. The amount of information for such students should also be reduced so that the student can explore learning content without getting cognitively overloaded and has more time to explore essential learning content without worrying about the rest. The structure of the exploration space is, however, a thought-provoking aspect. While a more structured exploration space will help a student with low working memory capacity, the structure itself will hinder the exploration activity which is expected to provide the students with navigation freedom to explore. Any changes in the structure will have both negative and positive impacts on the students with low working memory capacity which will cancel out each other, and therefore, there is no benefit in changing the structure of the exploration space. However, these students will benefit from more concrete information so that they can grasp the fundamental concepts first and then use them to generate higher-order concepts. Similarly, providing these students with the same learning content using different multimedia objects will give them an opportunity to choose those objects that work the best with their cognitive styles, contributing to their improved learning experience.

Let us take another example of the impact of low inductive reasoning ability on the exploration-based learning. Students with low inductive reasoning ability have difficulty in constructing concepts from examples. For such students, the number of exploration paths should increase so that the students have more opportunity to observe how concepts are applied in different examples and how they are different from other similar concepts. More familiarity with concepts applied in different contexts can help this process further. It would also enable better transfer of the learning to other contexts. At the same time, these students should be provided with diverse learning content and include the content with low relevance, so that they can have more diverse observations. The amount of learning content needs to be increased so as to provide these students with detailed explanations, which would help them in seeing the patterns in the examples more easily and grasp the underlying concepts better. The learning content for such students should be more structured so that the clues given in the structure will help them to build the mental model easily. Similarly, the learning content should be more concrete. The more examples and case studies the students have learned, the easier it will be for them to generalize and be able to transfer the learning outcomes to other contexts. Finally, the same learning content should be provided using different types of multimedia objects, so that the students can learn from those objects that suit their personal cognitive styles. This will improve the possibility that the concept being learned matches associatively and analogically to a previously learned concept, which in turn will improve the possibility of successful induction.

Reflection exercise

If a student has low working memory capacity and high associative learning skill, what kind of learning content should be given to that student in terms of the number of learning objects, relevance of the learning content, amount of learning content, structure of exploration space, level of concreteness of the content, and the same content being presented through different types of multimedia objects?

A representative scenario

Let us look at how adaptivity and personalization can help in he learning process in an exploration-based learning environment in a medical domain, particularly focusing on the learning of the structure and functionality of the human ear and associated diseases. The first step would be to determine the learning goals, in order to differentiate them from the students' interests. The learning goals in such scenarios would be to (a) understand the structure and functionality of the human ear; and (b) acquire appropriate skills in diagnosing and treating ear diseases. The next step will be to select and develop various types of multimedia objects. For example, hypertext can be used to describe the structure and functionality of the ear (goal a). Animations can be used to demonstrate the behavior of a healthy ear (goal a). Simulations can be used to allow students to experiment on the functionality of the ear (goal a) and explore for diagnosis and treatment of diseases (goal b). Students can be asked to sequence problems based on their level of competence (goal a) and diagnose and treat problems in certain order (goal b). Once the multimedia objects are available, the next step is to decide what actions are possible on each type of multimedia object. In this scenario, hypertext can be selected and students can trace their path. Students can interpret the action shown in the animations. They can change values of various parameters in the simulations and interpret the results. The problem ordering allows students to trace the path they took during problem solving and pinpoint at which step they encountered problems in the learning process.

The decision about the restrictions on various aspects of the learning process is next to ensure that the complexity and amount of learning content remains within the acceptable limits of a student's cognitive load capacity. In the current scenario, the number of multimedia objects can be controlled to support both goals a and b. The restriction on navigation paths within the learning environment will also serve both goals. On the other hand, control on the amount of presented information within each multimedia object will help towards the goal, while embedding information as the students progress in their diagnosis of diseases will help with the second goal.

The next step in providing adaptivity and personalization in the current scenario is to decide on how to enforce restrictions on various multimedia objects. Here are some examples:

- The concept of main path and excursions

  - *Current topic:* structure of middle ear
  - *Excursion:* to "physics of sound" unit
  - *Restrictions:* Only sound travel through the mechanical linkage of ossicles is presented. Information regarding sound transfer from air to water (related to the inner ear) and other similar information is not presented to maintain the context.

- Limiting information resources (for understanding the structure and functionality of the ear)

  - *Restrictions:* The domain material with only certain level of complexity is presented (for example, static pictures vs virtual reality scenarios)
  - *Deciding parameter(s):* Exploration experience, cognitive load

- Limiting exploration paths (for understanding the structure and functionality of the ear)

  - *Restrictions:* Restricting buttons, combo box choices, anchors/links to be used in exploring hypermedia to limit actions to select & trace operations
  - *Deciding parameter(s):* Exploration competence, knowledge level

- Embedding information (for acquiring skills to diagnose and treat diseases)

  - *Restrictions:* Providing scaffolding so as to decrease domain complexity with regard to student characteristics (for example, first allowing the students to semi-explore the disease development process in an animation wizard; then adding simulation capabilities to allow the full exploration; and, then adding extra simulation capabilities for diagnosis)
  - *Deciding parameter(s):* Exploration competence

Links

Lost in hyperspace: http://en.wikipedia.org/wiki/Lost_in_hyperspace

References

CARLA (2015). Scaffolding Techniques in CBI Classrooms. Retrieved January 10, 2015, from, www.carla.umn.edu/cobaltt/modules/strategies/scaffolding_techniques.pdf.

Cowen, N. (2000). The magical number 4 in short-term memory: A reconsideration of mental storage capacity. *Behavioral and Brain Sciences*, 24, 87–185.

Kashihara, A., Kinshuk, Oppermann, R., Rashev, R. & Simm, H. (1997). An Exploration Space Control as Intelligent Assistance in Enabling Systems. International Conference on Computers in Education Proceedings (Z. Halim, T. Ottmann & Z. Razak (Eds.)), AACE, VA, 114–121.

Kinshuk, Lin T. & Patel A. (2006). User Adaptation in Supporting Exploration Tasks in Virtual Learning Environments. In J. Weiss, J. Nolan, J. Hunsinger & P. Trifonas (Eds.), *The International Handbook of Virtual Learning Environments* (Vol. 1), Dordrecht, The Netherlands: Springer, 395–425.

Miller, G. A. (1956). The magical number seven, plus or minus two: Some limits on our capacity for processing information. *Psychological Review*, 63, 81–97.

Piaget, J. (1967). Logique et Connaissance scientifique, Encyclopédie de la Pléiade, Paris: Gallimard.

seven
Adaptivity and Personalization in Mobile and Ubiquitous Settings

In previous chapters, we have discussed many different scenarios where adaptivity and personalization can improve students' learning experiences. In this chapter, we shall look at the application of adaptivity and personalization in mobile and ubiquitous learning environments. In such environments, students are typically not in classrooms, rather they learn wherever they are, on their mobile devices, such as cellphones or tablets. Let us look at how these types of situations have emerged.

There was a time when there were no computers in classrooms. Computers were in separate computer labs and students used them for a very short time per week. Then, with the emergence of mobile devices, lots of different platforms evolved. Now virtually every student has some sort of laptop or mobile device. We also have students now working at home, doing their assignments, and even learning from home. Along with laptop computers, many other devices have come up, such as cellphones, handheld computers and iBooks. Various operating platforms have also emerged, such as Windows, Apple iOS, Android, and so on.

The environment has also changed. Before, learning used to be in a classroom environment. Students would come to the class and that is the only place learning would be expected to happen. But now, we have learning happening in all different places and there is increasing realization that learning is not restricted only to classrooms. Learning can happen wherever there is an opportunity. If I am sitting in a bus, I have some time, I just open my phone or my tablet and start reading something and learning can happen there. If I am in a café and I am talking to my friends and suddenly we need to find something, we just start our cellphones, pull up a search engine and start looking for the information. We do not wait for going to classrooms or going home. Learning is now happening in different environments. Even in airplanes, nowadays Internet connection is becoming available. With such widespread availability of Internet connectivity, lots of different learning opportunities are coming up in computer-based learning environments. When that happens, the next questions become: "How can we make sure that learning is actually happening?" and "Is the learning happening effectively?" So how can we make sure that learning is happening and happening effectively when students are not in the classroom, when they are wherever they happen to be?

Let us consider "What makes learning happen?" The success of the learning process in a computer-based learning environment depends on a number of factors. First of all, presentation of the domain knowledge to the students—how to present the concepts and associated content to the students. Say, if a student is learning at home on a large screen desktop computer and has good Internet bandwidth, then providing rich multimedia content, including large video files will create no problems. But if a student is learning on a cellphone with a limited data connection and the learning environment decides to deliver video content of say, 20 megabytes, then it would take so long to even download that video to the cellphone that the learning process will not only be completely disrupted but may also be very costly for the student. So, it becomes very important to adapt the presentation of domain knowledge to suit the situation, the device the student is using, and where the student is.

Another important factor is the student's progress in the learning process. If the student is learning very well, then the learning environment can start to give more complex learning content. But, if the student is having difficulty in understanding, then giving more complex content will only hinder the learning. The adaptivity and personalization mechanism must make sure that the learning content presented to the student matches with the student's level of understanding. The granularity of the learning content also needs to be considered. Granularity refers to in how much detail the content should be given to a student. For a student who is new to a topic, giving just the overview or simple information is important. Then, as a student starts to know more and more about the topic, more detailed content, at higher granularity can be provided.

Next is the consideration of device and user preference profiles. For example, if the student is accessing the computer-based learning environment through a cellphone with a small screen, or if the bandwidth is not very good, then checking these issues and providing content accordingly is important. So, if the environment detects that the student is learning through a cellphone with limited bandwidth, then it should not provide any large videos because it would be difficult to download them. Similarly, user preferences enable the learning environment to understand the student better, i.e., his/her competencies, preferences and other attributes. Maybe the student has a visual learning style, so he/she would like to see more videos and images, compared to another student who likes to read more. There are a number of attributes that are included in a user preference profile, and a good adaptivity and personalization mechanism seamlessly adapts to the individual student's profile anytime and anywhere. What it means is that a good adaptive and personalized learning environment always checks where the student is, who the student is, what the student is trying to do, and on what device the student is trying to learn, and based on that, provides correct learning content, correct introduction, correct presentation, correct navigation, and so on.

How can we provide such kind of adaptation and personalization in mobile devices? Since mobile devices come in all shapes and sizes, have different operating systems, and support different functionality, we need a mechanism that can provide adaptivity and personalization across different types of devices. Let us discuss an adaptation and personalization framework for multiplatform environments. The idea is to find how the learning environment can adapt in different kinds of situations. So, if there is a student who is currently using a cellphone, the learning environment should know that at this point, the student is using a cellphone, and therefore provides whatever works on a cellphone. Then, if the same student goes home and starts using a desktop computer with a big screen and with high bandwidth, the learning environment should start giving rich multimedia content, such as videos etc., because now the student can handle that. The multiplatform framework should take care of such adaptation. The framework identifies what the environmental factors are that affect learning in such multiplatform environments? The framework then takes care of different parameters that affect learning in different kinds of environments. An example multiplatform framework is discussed in Goh and Kinshuk (2009).

In multiplatform environments, computer-based learning environments need to serve various requirements of a wide array of mobile devices without having to duplicate the services and content on the server side. What it means is that the learning environment should not try to make separate copies of the content to suit each type of mobile device. The learning environment should have only one instance of the content, and the adaptivity and personalization mechanism of the learning environment should customize that content to different devices in real time, based on different criteria. For example, when the learning environment detects that a student is using a cellphone on a data connection, it should not provide movies due to limited bandwidth available on data connections, and large images since it would be very difficult to view them on a small device. It should only give the student what will work on a small screen.

There are five distinct dimensions that the multiplatform framework needs to consider: the content dimension, the user model dimension, the device dimension, the connectivity dimension, and the coordination dimension. The framework is not exhaustive and there may be other aspects that need consideration, but these five dimensions cover a majority of the considerations needed in multiplatform environments.

The content dimension includes criteria such as how the content is organized and at what granularity, what kinds of learning modules are included, and what kinds of pedagogy need to be provided. This dimension represents the actual context and application of knowledge, where the learning is happening and what content is available. It includes things like course modules, such as how many parts there are in the course, chapters, sections, and so on; the level of difficulty of the content so that the environment can select the correct level of difficulty for the individual student; and the variety of multimedia representations available, such as text, audios, videos, and animations.

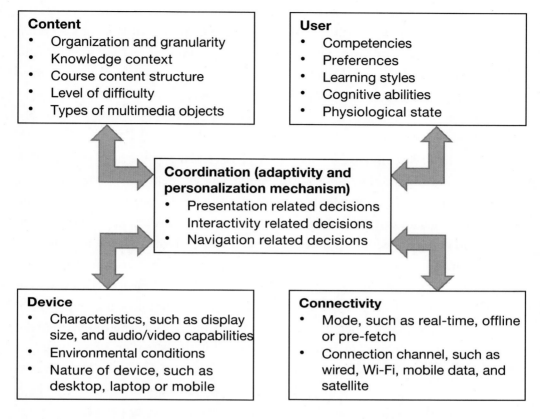

Content
- Organization and granularity
- Knowledge context
- Course content structure
- Level of difficulty
- Types of multimedia objects

User
- Competencies
- Preferences
- Learning styles
- Cognitive abilities
- Physiological state

Coordination (adaptivity and personalization mechanism)
- Presentation related decisions
- Interactivity related decisions
- Navigation related decisions

Device
- Characteristics, such as display size, and audio/video capabilities
- Environmental conditions
- Nature of device, such as desktop, laptop or mobile

Connectivity
- Mode, such as real-time, offline or pre-fetch
- Connection channel, such as wired, Wi-Fi, mobile data, and satellite

FIGURE 7.1 Multiplatform framework for computer-based learning environments

The user model dimension includes the information about individual students, such as competencies, preferences, learning styles, cognitive abilities and physiological state. The competency model includes up-to-date information about how much the student knows about a particular topic, how much he/she knows about other topics related to the current topic, and if the student has already learned the topic before, when was the last time the student learned this topic and has there been any knowledge decay since then. All competence related items such as modules already completed, marks obtained in each module, time taken to complete each module, date of last access, etc. are part of the user model. The user preferences include interface related parameters, such as colours, navigation preferences, and preferred difficulty level. The user model also includes learning styles such as the students' attitudes towards various types of learning activities, reflection capabilities, types of content, tendency to first look at an overview or details, and so on. The cognitive abilities in the user model include information about individual student's working memory capacity, associative learning skills, inductive reasoning ability and other mental abilities (Lin and Kinshuk, 2008). The physiological state includes information about students' physical parameters, such as heart rate, skin temperature, pupil dilation and so on that can be used to analyze stress levels, tiredness, and other similar symptoms.

The device dimension looks at the characteristics of the device the student is using and the conditions in which that device is being used. For example, a student may be using a desktop computer at a fixed location, such as at home or in a laboratory. These devices are generally high-end devices with large screen and high bandwidth. Another situation is where students use mobile devices, which they can carry in their pockets and take anywhere they want. While these devices provide learning opportunities at the instant a student needs and enable contextual learning, they are typically small and do not have high bandwidth. These devices are generally people's personal devices and are customized to the individual student's personal taste. There is another situation where a student is mobile and uses a fixed device in a public location, such as an Internet café. While these devices are typically high-end, with large monitors and high bandwidth, they are aimed to be used by large number of people, and therefore are not customizable to individual student's requirements. The device dimension also looks at the characteristics of individual devices, such as device type and its capabilities, for example, can it run java programs, does it have a camera, can it run Flash programs, and so on. The device dimension also looks at various capabilities of the devices, such as how large is the display, what kind of audio capability it has, does it have multi-language capability, how much memory it has, what kind of bandwidth it is currently using, and so on. For example, if a student is on Wi-Fi, he/she would have better bandwidth than someone is using mobile data. This dimension also checks whether the device can accept cookies, since the adaptivity and personalization mechanism of the learning environment may need information from cookies to be able to customize the content. Type of operation platform is another consideration for device dimension.

Next is the connectivity dimension, which looks at how the device being used by the student connects to online resources. There are three different modes for connectivity. The first one is real-time online, where the device is connected to the Internet at the time of learning. Next is off-line, where the device is not connected to the Internet at the time of learning. For example, if a student is going to travel by plane where it is known in advance that there will be no connection, he/she can synchronize the device to get content on his or her device before starting the travel. This way, the learning resources will be available during off-line mode. The third mode is called pre-fetching, which is used in those situations where there is a connection, but it is unreliable. In such situations, as and when the learning environment detects an unreliable connection, it first analyzes what content would be required by the students in the next learning activities and then attempts to pre-fetch that content when it can get the connectivity. That way, when the device loses the connectivity, the learning environment already has the content needed by the student to continue the learning process. The adaptivity and personalization mechanism of the learning environment therefore needs to analyze what learning content the student would need for subsequent learning activities. For example, if a student is currently learning Unit 2, then the next learning activity could be the quiz for Unit 2. The adaptivity and personalization mechanism can analyze the likelihood of the student's performance in the quiz, based on the student's performance till now and in recent actions, and determine whether to pre-fetch content for Unit 3 or more explanatory remedial content for Unit 2. In that way, when the learning environment does not have internet connection, it would already have the learning content for the student.

Another component of the connectivity dimension is the channel, which indicates the medium through which the student's device is connected to the Internet. Examples of the channel include wired connection, Wi-Fi, satellite connection, and so on. Let us take the example of satellite connection. While satellite connections are quite powerful and available in wider geographical areas, they typically have longer delays, which can be problematic in real-time communication. For example, if the learning activity includes real-time audio conversation between the student and the teacher or between two students, then delays of 5 to 10 seconds, which are normal in satellite-based connections, after every time a student or teacher talks would result in a very bad conversation experience. This may not be as problematic if the interaction was through text chat, as people are more patient in text chat as they accept that writing text takes more time than speaking. So, if the learning environment has information about the type of channel used for Internet connectivity, the adaptivity and personalization mechanism can suggest the activities and interaction options accordingly.

Next is the coordination dimension. The coordination dimension is the central decision making component which acts by using information from all the other dimensions. It is the primary component of the adaptivity and personalization mechanism of the learning environments. It is composed of the logic in the form of the programming inside the learning environments. For example, it decides what kind of presentation should be given to the student, based on the device being used by the student, the bandwidth available, and so on? How should the content be transformed? For example, if the content is all in a big page, the coordination dimension can divide it into smaller pages so it can fit better on a cellphone. Another example is interactivity, where a decision is made regarding whether to enable voice chat or to recommend text chat. It also decides what kind of navigation is suitable in a particular situation. For example, if the device that the student is using does not have any physical keys but only an onscreen keyboard, then the learning content and activities will be restricted to only those that do not require physical navigation keys. So, depending on the information available from other dimensions, the coordination dimension makes various decisions about learning content and activities to be recommended to the students. In a sense, the coordination dimension acts like a brain of the learning environment. It coordinates everything.

Test your understanding

1. Explain the role mobile devices can play in improving the learning experience.
2. How can different learning styles of students influence students' learning experiences?
3. In what situation can pre-fetching the content help in the learning process?

Multiplatform adaptation framework for learning environments

Let us now look at how a multiplatform adaptation framework can be used in the actual implementation of a learning environment. For this purpose, we shall look at another framework that provides practical guidelines for adaptation in multiplatform environment. Qing Tan and colleagues looked at the adaptation with particular focus on various mobile situations (Tan, Zhang, Kinshuk, & McGreal, 2012). Their framework takes the conceptual understanding to the level of implementation by analyzing various parameters that influence learning, and how adaptivity and personalization mechanism can be implemented in mobile situations. There are five factors considered in the framework: a student's personal attributes, a student's location, the time of learning, the device being used for learning, and the content needed for the current learning process. Let us see how this framework works. We must first identify who the student is. Next, in what context is this student learning? In what kind of situation is this student currently learning and what kind of structure needs to be provided to support learning in that situation? Next, what is the time when learning is taking place and what kind of device is the student using? Based on these parameters, the framework assembles dynamic content to provide to the student.

To implement the framework, we need to identify, what are the challenges facing the development of multiplatform adaptive learning environment. This requires looking at different contexts from the learning perspective. The key strategies are to identity and normalize context information based on efficient fusion of the context-aware data regarding student, location, time and device dimensions, in order to provide appropriate content. All these different dimensions have their own characteristics, priorities and other parameters. The designers of multiplatform adaptive learning environments need to combine these parameters from different dimensions to provide effective learning. The framework uses semantic-based context constraints for this purpose using composable ontology models. What it means is there are different ontology models for different parameters which are combined together using semantic information to provide proper learning content to the individual students.

Let us see how does this ontology-based approach works. It uses predefined metadata models of the learning contents, for example, learner model, contact information, device profile, and so on. It takes information from those models and filters it to the current situation. For example, it identifies what are various possibilities at a particular time, what kind of content is possible on a particular type of device, what kind of content will suit a student who has a certain level of competency, and so on. It then combines that filtered information to identify the most suitable content. It basically retrieves structured and unstructured learning materials and generates personalized, just-in-time, and location-aware learning content or an adaptive "filter". In other words, it takes all the content and then it tries to figure out, "OK, at this location this content will work, at this time this content will work, on this device this content will work, . . ." That is how it comes up with what is finally possible. Then the learning environment can provide that content to the student.

Next we shall discuss the creation of content. The first approach is to manually create semantic learning contents, by manually identifying all these different parameters. It is not an easy approach, but in some situations that may be the only possibility. The second approach is to take advantage of pre-existing learning objects. There are lots of learning objects available in various data banks or learning content repositories. In this approach, content developers develop shareable ontology using learning objects standards, and then identify what works on certain mobile services, to make those learning objects widely accessible. That way, those objects can be used by anyone who has access to the learning environment. The aim in this case is to conduct bottom-up development of the ontology for personalized learning objectives, using learning context information and the constraints imposed by various dimensions of the framework, namely time constraints, location constraints, device constraints, learner constraints, and content constraints.

The third approach is to develop a software and knowledge retrieval mechanism that can automatically identify appropriate learning content. This approach uses adaptive filters, where the adaptivity and personalization mechanism of the learning environment filters from all the collected information to automatically identify which learning objects will work at what time, at what kind of location, for which student, and on what device, and based on that assembles a set of learning objects to give to the individual student.

We shall now look at the examples of each dimension of the framework. The first dimension is time. A good example to illustrate the time dimension is the National Museum of American History in Washington, D.C. in United States.

This building has particular characteristics that make it interesting for students from many disciplines. This building collects, preserves and displays the heritage of the United States in the areas of social, political, cultural, scientific and military history. It also has a unique architectural significance. Since it is located on National Mall that has traditional architecture, it was designed to blend that traditional focus with more modern design which could reflect the technological and cutting-edge aspect of the museum. So, students of architecture and students of building sciences can go and look at this building to learn from this unique architectural aspect. At the same time, students majoring in social sciences, law, political sciences, and many other disciplines will find many important artefacts and documents in this building that are useful for their studies. Now, this building typically opens at 10 am and closes at 5:30 pm. So, if there is a student who wants to look at the artefacts or documents to learn from them, then the adaptive and personalized learning environment will check whether there is enough time for this purpose before the building closes that day. In such a situation, the environment may notify the student something like "Oh! There is a document inside that building that is very useful for you, but it is already 5:00 pm and the building will close at 5:30 pm. It is better to learn something else right now and go to that building tomorrow morning when it opens at 10 am." On the other hand, for a student of architecture or building sciences, the environment will notify something like "Even though it is 5:00 pm you can still go there because you only need to see the outside. You can go even now and I can navigate how you go there." So, depending on the time, the same environment will recommend something to one type of student, and something else to another type of student.

The next dimension is location, which enables the adaptivity and personalization mechanism to provide customized learning experiences based on students' locations. It also enables the learning environment to take advantage of unplanned movements and travels of students. When a student happens to be at a location where a local artefact can be useful to the student's current learning goals, the environment can notify the student, something like "Since you are here today, let me tell you about a place where you can learn really well about this particular topic. If you have some free time, I can guide you there." If the student agrees, the environment can navigate the student and start giving advice for learning about the local content. Such "opportunistic learning" is possible through the consideration of the time dimension.

The next dimension is the device. Different types of devices have different characteristics and functionalities. For example, some devices can run Flash content and some not, whereas other devices can run java programs. Some devices may run JavaScript, or some devices may allow cookies. All such differences in the devices affect what kind of content, navigation and interaction are possible for a particular student.

The next dimension is content, which enables the learning environment to decide what type of learning objects can be provided to the student from those that are available in that particular environment, what learning activities the student can undertake to learn that particular content, what kind of instruction should be provided for those learning activities, and what kind of pedagogy will best suit for that instruction.

Then the next dimension is the personal characteristics of the students. Different students have different requirements. They have different learning abilities, different preferences, and different learning styles. Also, the aim of learning is different for each individual student. So, the learning environment needs to decide what kind of content should be given to each individual student, based on personal characteristics.

Test your understanding

Create an example scenario of adaptive learning where at least three of the five dimensions of the adaptation framework are used together to provide adaptivity: time, location, device, content and student characteristics.

Reflection

This exercise asks you to create the scenario manually. Now, if a learning environment had to make these adaptations itself, then what kind of rules could be created that the environment could use to provide such adaption? Those rules can enable the environment to provide automatic adaptation. Your task is to write some of those rules so that the environment can do such adaptation itself.

Implementation of the framework

Now we shall look at how the framework can be implemented in adaptive and personalized learning environments. In such learning environments, the students access the learning content from different places, using a variety of devices, such as desktop or laptop computers at home or school, and mobile devices in outside places. The learning environment analyzes the location of the student and determines what physical learning resources are available at that location. However, to be able to identify the physical learning resources at a student's location, those resources need to be created. Since the student could be accessing the learning environment from anywhere, it is not possible for a teacher to create all the resources at every geographical location. These resources could be located anywhere in the world, and it is not possible for a teacher to go to every place. Therefore a better option is to adopt crowdsourcing, where the content can be created by anyone. For example, when a student, parent, or any other person finds a physical object that may be of educational interest, that person can take a picture of that object using his/her mobile device, add a description of it, and then upload that into the learning environment. The location coordinates are also attached to that object. Once such an object is submitted, it is authenticated by the teacher to verify its validity, usefulness and quality for the goals of the learning. The teacher can also edit the description provided by the person who uploaded the object and can add additional explanations, examples, and so on. Once the teacher has approved the object, it becomes available to the students as part of the learning content. As and when a student is in the geographical location where that object is located, the learning environment can create learning activities using that object and provide them to the student.

Such implementation is capable of supporting different types of learning processes. Let us take a look at one such example of observational and action-oriented learning. Observational learning is suitable in situations where the student is new to a topic and is trying to understand the basic knowledge. The learning environment provides various observation-based activities to the student to acquire fundamental concepts of the topic. Once the student starts to understand the topic, the learning environment leads the student to engage in various hands-on activities to obtain deeper understanding as well as skills associated with the topic. For observational learning, the learning environment needs to combine those aspects of various dimensions that can identify the appropriate learning content without a student's active participation in the process since the purpose is to provide observation. Therefore, the learning environment uses various "active techniques", such as Bluetooth and active radio frequency identification tags (Active RFIDs) that proactively announce their presence to the student device. Bluetooth modules have low power consumption. They are small in size, are relatively cheaper, and allow installation of a large number of devices in a target area. However, they do suffer with low data rate of only 1 mbps and are not very secure. Active RFIDs allow for digital read and write functions. They are miniature and can take diverse forms. They are environmentally resistant, are reusable, and have high penetration. They are however costly. The learning content attached to these types of active techniques is then discovered by the student's device automatically without requiring the student to actively search for it. Instead, the student's device can guide the student to the learning content. The student can simply observe and learn. Once the student gets some basic knowledge of the topic, the learning environment initiates action-oriented learning where the student explores various physical objects in the surroundings and engages in various hands-on activities to learn. Various passive techniques are used in this phase of learning. These techniques do not announce themselves. The students have to search for them in order to engage with the physical objects attached to them. For example, QR codes (short for Quick Response code, consisting of black square dots arranged in a square grid on a white surface and can be scanned using a simple mobile phone camera) can be attached to various physical objects. The students actively look for objects that have QR codes and scan those codes to find out about those objects. QR codes can be easily read by typically available mobile devices, as they are readable by typical cameras of mobile phones. They can contain a relatively large amount of information within a small printing area. They are also anti-fouling. However, they can only contain static data. Any change in the information would require creation of a new QR code.

A representative scenario

Student A in a remote working community is using a mobile phone to learn a certain topic. The phone is Wi-Fi, Bluetooth and GPS enabled. The content is being transferred to the phone via Wi-Fi through an access point from a server, which also contains the student's personal profile. The personal profile includes information about the student's previous learning history, competence levels in different subject areas, cognitive capabilities and other personal characteristics.

On this particular occasion, the learning environment, with the permission from the student, observes student A's current progress and infers that A is finding it difficult to progress in the current subject content. Using GPS tracking, the learning environment identifies the student's position and then checks to see if it can track any other students nearby who have given permission to be tracked and are studying at a similar level in the subject content and may wish to join this student to make an ad-hoc study group. The learning environment brings these students together at one place through GPS-based navigation. Once the students are near enough to each other that they are within the Bluetooth range of each other, GPS tracking is switched off. The learning environment then identifies the surroundings of the students through analyzing location dimension. It then analyzes content dimension to create a generic multimedia-based problem to align with the students' physical environment. The learning environment then divides the problem into smaller pieces to match the number of students in the current study group. It then pushes out appropriate problem items to each student in the group by analyzing the student characteristics dimension. The students then discuss the problem face-to-face and by interacting with the problem pieces on each other's phones, try to solve their own pieces of the problem, and transfer intermediate solutions to other students' phone for further problem solving. The students then try to reach a conclusion through intensive dialog and collaborative learning. Once they have solved a problem, the archive of the interactions is sent back to the learning environment so that the individual profiles of the students can be updated and appropriate further content can be pushed out to the individual students for further learning, based on how each of them performed in the study group.

Learning activities

1. Create a fictional scenario by selecting a physical environment where different artefacts can help the students learning a history subject (for example, a museum, an art gallery, or some other similar place).

2. Select at least three functions available on your student's mobile device (such as Wi-Fi, camera, or similar).

3. Select a particular topic in history that your student wants to learn.

4. Identify at least five characteristics of your student, such as his/her competency level in that topic, the learning styles of the student, the level of working memory capacity, and so on.

5. Create a learning activity that your student can do in the physical environment you selected, on the mobile device with selected functionality for the topic your student wants to learn, matching with the student characteristics you have identified.

Share your ideas with your colleagues and ask them to critique. Provide feedback to your colleagues on their ideas in return.

Links

National Museum of American History—Smithsonian Institution: https://en.wikipedia.org/wiki/National_Museum_of_American_History

Resources

National Museum of American History—Smithsonian Institution: http://americanhistory.si.edu/

References

Goh, T. T., & Kinshuk (2009). E-learning Systems Content Adaptation Frameworks and Techniques. In M. Pagani (Ed.), *Encyclopedia of Multimedia Technology and Networking*, Hershey, PA: Information Science Reference, 460–468.

Lin T. & Kinshuk (2008). A Multiple-Portrayal-Network for Multiple Perspectives Inclusion in Cognitive-Trait-Model. *Journal of Intelligent Systems, 17* (4), 355–377 (ISSN 0334–1860)

Tan, Q., Zhang, X. K., Kinshuk, & McGreal, R. (2012). The 5R Adaptation Framework for Location-Based Mobile Learning Systems (In Chinese). Journal of Modern Distance Education Research, 117 (3), 91–96.

part three

PRACTICAL PERSPECTIVES WITH EXAMPLE APPLICATIONS

eight

Implementation Process of Adaptive and Personalized Learning Environments

We have so far looked at the application of adaptivity and personalization to support different aspects of learning. Now we shall look at how the adaptive and personalized learning environments can be implemented to support different types of learning requirements. We shall consider two situations: the environments supporting life-long learning, and the environments to facilitate synchronous remote collaboration activities.

Implementation of life-long learning environment with adaptivity and personalization

Let us look at an example of computer-based life-long learning environment with adaptivity and personalization, which uses symbolic representations to explain the concepts for the development of cognitive skills. It uses those capability of computers in which they are currently good for providing effective learning to the students. The environment does not pretend that it knows the students well. It also does not pretend that it can provide explanations like teachers can do. But what it does is that it tries to visualize concepts using symbolic representations. It uses a bottom-up approach and instead of trying to provide a comprehensive system that covers everything in the domain through a centralized all-encompassing knowledge base, the environment consists of various computer-based learning tools where each tool focuses on a small part of the domain. Each tool in the environment, while having major functionality of traditional intelligent tutoring systems (Figure 8.1), has therefore a very limited domain area. On the other hand, these tools are free-standing and they can work on their own. But at the same time, they can also be integrated with each other to provide more advanced learning.

The first principle used in the environment is to use computers and humans for what they are currently good at. The second principle is to use computers and computer-based tools in the overall learning environment, instead of treating computers themselves as the overall learning environments. The overall learning environment consists of the educational environment where computers and humans both play significant roles. Computer-based learning tools do not try to replace teachers. Teachers still control the overall educational process and they can use these tools for their benefit and for the benefit of

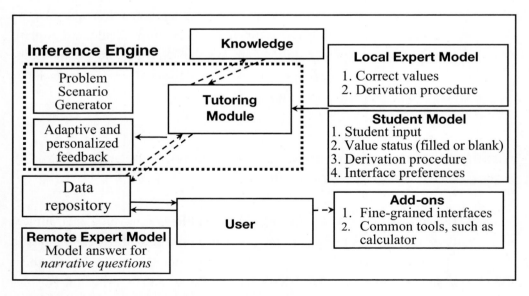

FIGURE 8.1 Major intelligent tutoring functionality

students. The third principle is to enable students to do what they can do themselves in the absence of a human teacher. The computer-based learning tools apply certain degrees of intelligence in the way that when a student requests help or support, the adaptivity and personalization mechanism kicks in for that particular student in that particular situation.

The fourth principle is that these tools are supposed to be used on mass scale. What that means is that these tools are not expected to help only those top 5% to 10% students, who are highly motivated and will successfully complete the learning process even without any such help, or those 5% to 10% students on the other extreme who are simply not ready for the current learning goals as they may not have the required prerequisites or may not have the basic skills to complete the learning process. These tools are expected to benefit from the economies of the scale by helping the majority of students in the middle range who require help and have potential to learn and succeed.

These computer-based learning tools treat the knowledge at three levels. The first level is the *introductory application level* that is based on very small units of domain concepts. At this level, the formation of the mental map of inter-related conceptual atoms takes place and the students learn how to use the basic tools of a discipline. For example, a tool may cover the concept of friction in a physics domain. The second level is *advance integration level* where the integration of various standalone computer-based learning tools takes place for more advance learning. The learning provided at this level is still simplistic. It does not assume that the environmental factors, the probabilities, or the actual realities of real-world environments are being considered. At this level, the learning is still of core concepts. The integration of various tools at this level happens in two ways: vertical integration and horizontal integration. Vertical integration involves a comparison of the results of multiple use of the same computer-based learning tool, for example, in a physics domain, comparing four springs of different dimensions or adding the effect of fatigue and creep. Horizontal integration employs multiple tools to solve a given problem, for example, the design of a safety valve for a steam boiler using computer-based learning tools for spring design, screw design and so on. The individual computer-based learning tools are used for various sub-tasks but a higher level application is used for holding and comparing the results of multiple instances of a tool, and linking various tools, to guide a student through the whole task. The third level is the *simulated real-world application level*, where the actual real world situations are simulated and the students learn to understand the behavioural and environmental contexts of the domain, where various real-world factors are introduced, such as fuzziness, openness of information, missing information, and probabilities. Actual environmental factors therefore start affecting the problem space.

The computer-based learning tools in the life-long learning environment project are mixed-initiative systems. Either student or tools can initiate the learning process. These tools have applied inference engine. What it means is that the domain knowledge is stored in a two-fold knowledge base—a local system and an overall global system. The local system provides content that is bound with pre-determined parameters. The overall global system enables more open-ended scenarios in the form of narrative questions. Such narrative questions require interpretation of data in order to figure out what the actual problem is. These types of questions have multiple variables, interlinked with each other, and as the students start to pick certain information in order to solve parts of the problem, other information becomes restrained. Such questions may also allow input of missing information, and the overall solution may change, based on the additional information. There is no pre-determined solution path for such questions. The learning tools follow the path students are taking and check whether students have correctly interpreted the information available and whether they have done correct analysis and calculations.

The tools contain two types of expert models: a local expert model and a remote expert model. The local expert model contains the local solution to the problem a student is attempting, whereas the remote expert model contains solutions based on the interpretation of the data. For example, if there was a problem, which was given to the student in narrative form the student is supposed to interpret the problem narrative in order to find the values of various variables, enter them in the tool interface and try to solve the problem. In such a scenario, there are two types of mistakes the student can make. First, operational mistakes, where some calculation is incorrect, which may be due to some misunderstanding of one or more interrelationships among any variables. The second type of mistake relates to the problem in correctly interpreting the narrative of the problem. If a student misinterpreted the narrative and entered the wrong values on the interface, then, even if the student applied all the relationships among the variables correctly, the answers will still be wrong. The combination of two types of expert models enables the tool to identify wrong interpretation and wrong understanding of interrelationships separately.

These computer-based learning tools are not intended to replace teachers but to complement by providing repetitive training opportunities to the students to gain mastery in the concepts taught by the teachers. The tools do not provide explanations that are more effectively provided by the teachers. These tools are for the teachers to mix and match with many other teaching aids teachers may want to use in different configurations to suit different teaching modes, such as classroom instruction, field experiments and distance learning mode.

Test your understanding

1. What are the four principles of the computer-based life-long learning environments?
2. What kind of learning takes place at the introductory application level?
3. What is the difference between vertical integration and horizontal integration of computer-based learning tools?

A representative scenario

Let us discuss a scenario from the domain of physics for students to learn about designing *close coil helical springs*. When designing such springs, there are a number of variables and relationships that need to be considered:

$T = W * D/2$ Torque = Axial Load * Mean Coil Diameter/2

$Z = (\pi /16) * d^3$ Section Modulus = $(\pi /16)$ * (Wire Diameter)^3

$\tau = T / Z$ Max. Shear Stress (*No fatigue*) = Torque / Section Modulus

$\delta = \theta * d/2$ Axial Deflection = Twist * Wire Diameter/2

$J = (\pi/32) * d^4$ Polar Second Moment of Inertia = $(\pi /32)$ * (Wire Diameter)^4

$\theta = (T*l) / (G*J)$ Twist = (Torque * Length of wire) / (*Modulus of Rigidity* * Polar Second Moment of Inertia)

Modulus of Rigidity (G) => Constant

Each of these variables can be calculated using different relationships, depending on what other variables are available in the network of variable relationships. For example, Torque (T) is related with eight variables (W, D, θ, G, J, l, τ and Z).

$$T = W * D / 2$$
$$T = θ * G * J / l$$
$$T = τ * Z$$

So, if the student enters a value for Torque and a value for Mean Coil Diameter (D), then the value for Axial Load (W) will become constrained. But if the student enters values for Axial Load and Mean Coil Diameter, then Torque will become constrained.

Other examples of relationships are:

$$Z = (π / 16) * d^3 \qquad J = (π/32) * d^4 \qquad θ = (T*l) / (G*J)$$
$$Z = T / τ \qquad J = T * l / (G * θ) \qquad θ = 2 * δ / d$$

By starting calculations through picking some variables as independent, other variables will become dependent. The computer-based learning tools provide the students with problem-solving interfaces where the students have the possibility to start the problem-solving process using any of the variables. As soon as the students enter a variable, the tool tries to calculate any other related variable. Since there are many possible ways to solve the problem, the tool will continue to identify which variables have become constrained, as the students continue to enter various variables. The tools allow flexible learning process. There is no fixed sequence of filling in the variables. Any value can be entered by the students any time, including values for any variables that have already become constrained, as long as the whole network of variables remains consistent. Correct values for variables are accepted even if any intermediate calculations are missing. However, if a student enters a wrong value for any variable whose value has already been determined due to previously entered other variables, the adaptivity and personalization mechanism kicks in for providing feedback.

If the student is trying to learn a complex concept, and he/she encounters problems, then the mechanism helps by advising him/her to carry out necessary intermediate steps before attempting to calculate the complex concept in question. The mechanism uses granularity negotiation process for providing help for complex concepts. It distributes these concepts at different granularities, some at their basic granularity, at their basic state, where no further division can take place. That means if the student did not calculate the variable properly, it would mean the student does not know the basic concept. But there are variables where the students require understanding of various other intermediate variables or concepts. In those cases, the mechanism would break down the granularity to a finer level if the student did not understand that at a higher level. In this particular scenario, the network is for designing *close coil helical spring* which is the atom. Within that atom, there are smaller concepts, such as torque, axial load, and so on.

This approach, therefore, benefits from the strengths of both teachers and tools of the trade. Students are expected to learn the basic concepts of the domain from the teacher and then use the tools for problem solving, repetitive training, and for integrating the overall domain competence by bringing various knowledge pieces together in different scenarios. For example, the tool can provide the students with a scenario of a fixed length pipe for which a close coil helical spring needs to be designed, or a turbine which does not have any length restriction but has fixed diameter, or a close-coil helical spring is needed for a platform that must withstand certain weight, and so on. Therefore, such tools can help students to apply their theoretical knowledge in various contexts to improve their domain competence.

These tools focus on a *'what to do next?'* paradigm rather than a *'how did I come here?'* Rather than analysing why the student made a mistake, or what learning path he/she followed, these tools look at the current situation of the student and attempt to analyse what the student should do next and what are the efficient pathways for doing that. Coupled with adaptive and personalized feedback, which prevents any mistakes in the first place, this paradigm keeps on reinforcing the correct connections through the network of interrelationships.

The feedback from the adaptivity and personalization mechanism is provided by considering what the student is doing and how he/she has performed. If the student's input is correct, the mechanism does not intervene. However, as and when the student makes a mistake, the mechanism then checks whether the value of the concept related to the current step in the problem-solving process can be calculated from the values of already derived concepts in the current problem, or does it require calculation of the values of some intermediate concepts before the value of the current concept could be calculated. If intermediate values are required, the mechanism advises the student to first calculate those before proceeding further. However, if the value of the concept related to the current step in the problem-solving process can be calculated from the values of already derived concepts in the current problem, the mechanism provides scaffolding. It first simply informs the student that the answer is wrong and asks to calculate again. If the student still makes a mistake, the mechanism provides details of the relationship that the student should be using to calculate that value. If the student still does not understand, the mechanism shows the actual calculations for that value. If for some reason, the student still fails to enter the correct answer, the mechanism enters the correct answer for the student and suggests that the student learn the concept again. If the student wants to attempt another problem scenario instead of learning the concept again, the tool allows for that, since the assumption is that the student will encounter similar problem-solving process in another scenario and will learn by practice.

Learning activities

1. In the representative scenario in the previous section, there are a number of variables. Write down those variables on paper in the form of a concept map.
2. Link as many variables to each other by identifying the relationship between them using the formulae mentioned in the previous section.
3. Then, assign any numeric values for any three variables and try to calculate all other remaining variables. Note down which variables you were able to calculate and which could not be calculated.
4. Try step three a few more times by assigning any numeric values for any three variables other than the combinations you have already tried, and see if there is a combination that allows you to calculate all other variables.

Share your findings with your colleagues and ask them to critique. Provide feedback to your colleagues on their findings in return.

Implementation of synchronous remote collaboration-based adaptive and personalized learning environments

We shall now look at another example of adaptive and personalized learning environment implementation, this time to facilitate synchronous remote collaboration. In today's global environment, remote collaboration is not an exception, rather it is becoming a norm. There are many reasons for this. For example, organizations are realizing the need to augment their available expertise by temporarily tapping into external experts. Globalization also means that employees need to better understand different cultures, talk to people from different parts of worlds effectively, be it talking to their customers, suppliers or other stakeholders, and be able to express themselves successfully to others.

Many different approaches have been used by organizations for remote collaboration using technology, and majority of those approaches have been asynchronous in nature where people from different parts of the world typically communicate with each other in writing without interacting in real time. In such scenarios, people have an opportunity to spend time to assemble their thoughts, write them down, go through them again and revise as needed. Group learning and collaborative problem solving are among various learning situations where remote asynchronous collaboration has been successful. However, such asynchronous situations do not allow for real time dialog among remote partners and lack immediate clarifications from the participants, which is important for better understanding of each other.

On the other hand, synchronous remote collaboration requires consideration of various issues that can hinder successful collaboration. The first step in the implementation of adaptive and personalized learning environment to support remote synchronous collaboration requires understanding of those issues. The first category of those issues are student related. In synchronous remote collaboration, students from different parts of the world need to be present at the same time making it difficult for some due to differences in time zones. Different languages can create barriers in understanding. Students from different cultures may have difficulty in understanding each other due to their cultural differences. For example, red colour is treated as the colour of victory and prosperity in some cultures and colour of conflict in others. Another important student-related issue is the differences in expectations of students from remote areas.

Another category of issues that requires consideration is technological issues. Synchronous remote collaboration requires much higher bandwidth compared to its asynchronous counterpart, as all participants need to be present at the same time. Special technological solutions are needed to support real-time interaction among the students. The situation may be further complicated if not all students are using the same type of operating systems on the computers to connect to each other. In such situation, support for heterogeneous environments becomes critical. With the emergence of mobile technologies, consideration for both mobile and non-mobile scenarios is required as well as a mix of both, since it is possible that some of the students may be mobile at the time of interaction whereas other students may not be.

The issues discussed above may lead to problems in synchronous remote collaboration, which can create misunderstandings among the students, affecting the learning process. The adaptivity and personalization mechanism therefore becomes crucial to ensure effective interaction among the students.

A learning environment that supports synchronous remote collaboration through adaptivity and personalization needs to deal with misunderstandings among the collaborating students in a heterogeneous communication environment, including desktop and mobile devices, through user profiling techniques, such as a cognitive profile, a preference profile and a competency profile of the students. It needs to deal with the misunderstanding by correctly analyzing the situation of the collaboration. The situation theory of Jon Barwise and Robin Cooper is particularly helpful for this purpose (1991). According to the situation theory, the objects in the world do not exist on their own. They have properties and they stand in relation to one another. Parts of the world are clearly recognized through common sense and can be described in language even if they are not clearly separated from the rest of the world. These parts are situations. The learning environment needs to be able to analyze various personal factors, environmental conditions and differences among individual students that can result in various misunderstandings, creating these situations.

Keith Devlin identified several of them (2008). For example, events and episodes are situations in time. Scenes are visually perceived situations. Changes are sequences of situations, and facts are situations described through language. Let us look at how the situations relate to misunderstandings in synchronous remote collaboration. Personal situations occur due to the effect of an individual student's personal profile, such as competency and biomedical conditions. Global situations result from the effects of other people and particular meeting/discussion situations. For example, in a video-based collaboration meeting, if a participating student is reading emails on the side and laughs because of some funny content in the email, it could be seen and misinterpreted by other participants. Such wrong interpretation of gestures that resulted from another context of a participant can contribute to misunderstandings. The third category of situations is related to devices and can result from the effect of devices used by the participating students.

Let us now consider how to analyze misunderstandings through an example. Misunderstandings can occur if a participating student in a synchronous remote collaboration misses the context of the conversation. This happens when the student has no previous knowledge of the subject matter being discussed to make association between the current discussion and the previous knowledge. The situation will become even more critical if the student had low domain competence. Such a student will show a puzzled look which can be captured through camera. He or she would feel stressed, resulting in variability in heart rate. That student would perhaps also ask for some background information, which can be analyzed by microphone. So, a combination of various sensors can help in determining what kind of misunderstanding the student has. The adaptivity and personalization mechanism can evaluate the situation and check the student's user profile for past performance to assess low domain competence. It can then conclude that the misunderstanding is due to missing context and provide appropriate support to the student.

Another example of misunderstanding is when a student missed hearing some part of the conversation during a synchronous remote collaboration. This situation will be even more critical if there were external disturbances in the student's surrounding environment and if the student has low information processing speed. In such a situation, the student will probably interrupt the ongoing collaboration activities by using phrases such as "what?" or "I beg your pardon?" These interruptions can be picked up by the microphone. He or she may also show certain expressions of confusion on his or her face, which the camera can detect. The student may also show signs of stress, resulting in a variable heart rate. The microphone will also pick up the external disturbances. The adaptivity and personalization mechanism can evaluate the situation. It can also check the student profile in order to assess the student's low information processing speed. It will then conclude that the misunderstanding is due to missing parts of the conversation and provide appropriate support to the student.

As you can see, various input sources provide different kinds or information that can help the adaptivity and personalization mechanism to better understand what kind of misunderstandings are happening in certain situations. The first type of input sources relate to the profile of the students. For example, the background information of the students can be acquired by directly questioning the students. This kind of information does not change and can be used long term after acquisition unless any factual errors need to be corrected at a later stage. Areas of the student's interest can also be asked directly and they also remain valid for longer periods in the context of study. Various wearable sensors can also provide information about a student. For example, emerging smart watches, various fitness trackers and even new mobile phones can measure heart rate, skin temperature and perspiration count. Head movement and body movement can also be detected through an accelerometer sensor available in these devices. Such data is received continuously and is dynamic in nature. Past history of this data can help in understanding patterns of the student's physiological condition. A student's cognitive profile can be acquired by observing the student's interactions during a synchronous remote collaboration and analysing any emerging patterns. A cognitive profile includes information on various cognitive traits, such as the student's working memory capacity, associate learning skills, inductive reasoning ability, and so on. While the levels of these cognitive traits remain constant over a long period of time (if someone has high working memory capacity, it will not become low within a short period of time unless some unexpected event, such as an accident, happens), the interactions will provide information on a continuous basis, which can help in making a more reliable assessment of the student's cognitive profile. Another component of the student's profile is the student's understanding level, as identified by the source of the knowledge. In a synchronous remote collabora-tion, it is very important to ascertain that the student understood what others said and had the same understanding that was intended by the person who said it, so that there are no misunderstandings.

The next input source relates to the profile of the device used by the student during a synchronous remote collaboration. This includes the information about the type of device: whether it is a mobile device or a fixed computer, the size of screen, and other information that can affect the synchronous remote collaboration activities. It also includes information on the reliability of the bandwidth, which can affect the collaboration. The profile of the device also includes information on the available sensors that can be used to detect the situation, for example, camera, microphone, speakers, headphones, location sensor, accelerometer, and so on. Physiological sensors, such as a heart rate sensor and an oxygen level sensor, are also becoming available in recent wearable devices, such as smart watches and newer mobile phones.

Various biomedical conditions can be identified and measured through various sensors. For example, the tone of the voice can be detected by microphone. Increase in heart rate variation, combined with decrease in skin temperature and increase in perspiration, indicate signs of sleepiness. Heart rate increases when the student is concentrating on something. Tiredness and tenseness can be identified by checking whether the skin temperature and level of perspiration are increasing, the eye view is becoming narrow and if eye movement has slowed down. The level of excitement can be measured by loudness of the voice through microphone, the increase in perspiration and the increase in body movement which can be measured by the accelerometer. Gestures, such as yawning can be identified through camera and a decrease in heart rate.

The student's textual and visual input, as observed through keyboard typing or drawing on a sketch board or whiteboard during a synchronous remote collaboration also provide important input to the adaptivity and personalization mechanism to understand the student's needs.

Once the misunderstandings are identified or a potential risk of misunderstanding in certain situation is detected, there are a number of ways in which the adaptivity and personalization mechanism can support the students. For example, if the adaptivity and personalization mechanism identifies that the student has low short term memory (from the cognitive profile of the student), and that he/she is using a mobile device (from the device profile), the mechanism can present keywords from the current discussion on the student's device interface to ensure that the student does not lose track of the discussion. Based on the student's preference for the medium (from the student's profile) and whether the student is stationary, walking, or is in a vehicle (from the location sensor), the keywords can either be presented as text or through audio (e.g., when on the move, text messages may not be suitable).

If the mechanism identifies that there is a risk of the student misunderstanding the essence of the current discussion, it can ask a summary of the discussion from the listener student and get it checked by the speaker student to verify the understanding. The mechanism can also prompt a message either by flashing a pop-up window on the student's screen or by a voice prompt if it detects that the student is not attentive towards the collaboration activity, particularly when any of the areas of student's interest are mentioned in the current discussion or if the student's name is mentioned.

To summarize, misunderstandings in a synchronous remote collaboration can create significant obstacles in the way of successful interaction, leading to problems in the learning process. An adaptive and personalized learning environment therefore needs to utilize the technology effectively in order to not only help the student in case a misunderstanding occurs, but also prevent the misunderstandings from happening by analyzing the situation of collaboration in real time.

Test your understanding

1. What is the difference between asynchronous remote collaboration and synchronous remote collaboration?
2. Describe any two causes of misunderstandings in synchronous remote collaboration.
3. How can the differences in students' cultures contribute to misunderstandings?

References

Barwise, J., & Cooper, R. (1991). Simple Situation Theory and its graphical representation. *DYANA Report R2.1.C*, 38–74, retrieved August 8, 2015, from www.ling.gu.se/~cooper/ekn.ps.

Devlin, K. (2008). Situation Theory and Situation Semantics, retrieved August 8, 2008, from www.stanford.edu/~kdevlin/HHL_SituationTheory.pdf.

nine

Adaptive and Personalization of Learning in Various Contexts

Learning in different scenarios requires consideration of different parameters. Success of learning in different scenarios therefore depends on appropriate application of adaptivity and personalization to suit the context of that particular scenario. In this chapter, we shall discuss the application of adaptivity and personalization in different contexts, with particular examples of cognitive skills based learning and learning through simulations.

Adaptivity and personalization in cognitive skills acquisition

Let us start with discussing the application of adaptivity and personalization in the acquisition of cognitive skills. Previously, we discussed two major components of domain competence: theoretical knowledge and skills. Skills can be further classified into physical skills (or sensory motor skills) and cognitive skills. Physical skills are those skills that require some physical action. These skills can be acquired by hands-on practice of physical tasks. Cognitive skills, on the other hand, are those skills that are inside someone's mind. These can also be seen as decision making skills. We shall first look at an established theoretical framework that has been found effective for providing cognitive skills, and then we shall see how we can use that framework to create computer-based systems to provide learning for cognitive skills.

In 1989, Allan Collins, John Seely Brown and Susan Newman proposed a cognitive apprenticeship approach for the learning of cognitive skills. Unlike physical skills that can be practiced by watching someone else do certain physical tasks and copying those actions, cognitive skills are difficult to copy as they remain inside the human mind. For example, if a carpenter wants to create a table, then he would need to first take a decision about which wood he should use. How would he make such a decision? Inside his mind, he may think about where the table may be used, how strong the table needs to be, in what kind of environment that table will be, what kind of price range that table needs to be in, and so on. The carpenter will need to use a variety of factors for deciding which kind of wood should be used for the table. If we are standing near the carpenter and he is thinking about that, it would be impossible for us to understand the reasons behind his decisions just by observing him.

Now let us compare that with physical skills. Say, if we are standing in a kitchen and some people are cooking something, we can learn a lot just by looking at them and watching which different ingredients they are adding, which pots they are using, how long they are heating something, how long they are frying, and so on. As you can see, physical skills can be observed. It is not possible to observe cognitive skills in a similar manner because they remain hidden inside human mind.

Cognitive skills through cognitive apprenticeship approach

So how do we support learning of cognitive skills through computers? First of all, let us look at the cognitive apprenticeship approach that specifically aims at fostering cognitive skills. There are three main steps of this approach. The first step is "modelling", where students watch experts doing certain tasks, observe those action patterns, and in the process, develop their own cognitive model of the task. So when experts are doing some action, the students have the opportunity to reflect on questions like "Why did the expert do that?" or "Why did the expert behave that way?" So, the "modelling" step enables the students to study the task patterns of experts to develop their own cognitive model.

The "modelling" step primarily consists of observation. However, observation is not enough for cognitive skills development. As we discussed earlier, cognitive skills are in the mind, and it is not possible to see inside the mind. But, it is possible to see the results of those cognitive skills in terms of what is happening in the real world (the expert's actions). The students can then reflect on the cause of those actions to reach the possible decisions behind those actions, and then try to solve the problem themselves. At that moment, the experts can start to give feedback. This step of cognitive apprenticeship approach is called "coaching". In coaching, students try some activities, and the experts watch and give feedback. For example, the experts may say "Not this wood. Remember that the table will be used outside. So, we need to use the wood that will not get damaged in the rain, or in the strong sun, or in the wind." Experts provide feedback on all aspects of the tasks the students are doing, and students use that feedback to correct and refine their activities. Experts may also provide tutorials on certain topics if they see any particular misconceptions or missing conceptions. They may also provide more advanced knowledge to those students who are progressing well in their learning process. The more the students practice and the more feedback they get, the more competent they start to become in taking right decisions about those activities.

As the amount of mistakes and errors start to reduce, the feedback also starts to fade. When the experts see that the students have acquired the appropriate cognitive skills to make the right decisions, they do not need to give much feedback afterwards. This is where the third step of the cognitive apprenticeship approach, namely "fading", comes in. The tutorial activity is gradually reduced as the students start to improve their performance.

Test your understanding

1. What is the difference between physical skills and cognitive skills?
2. What are the three steps of cognitive apprenticeship approach?

Real life scenarios of cognitive skills acquisition

Let us analyze in more detail the real-life scenario of cognitive apprenticeship approach in the carpentry domain that we discussed earlier. Let us assume, there is a young person who goes to an expert carpenter to learn carpentry. What will the carpenter do? The carpenter will probably say something like, "Do you want to learn carpentry? OK. Come here and watch what we are doing, and help us whenever we ask". Sometimes the carpenter will say something like, "Give me a hammer" or "Give me that piece of wood". Basically, the carpenter will ask this apprentice to do small things here and there, since this apprentice does not yet have any skills. By just being there in that carpenter's workshop, the apprentice will start to understand the language of the discipline. He/she will observe that there are different types of woods, what a particular type of wood is called, what are the different tools used by different people in the carpenter's workshop, which tool is used most often by whom and for what purpose, and so on.

Then in time, the apprentice will start to gain some basic understanding. Once the carpenter feels that the apprentice has achieved some level of understanding, he will start to say something like, "Help me make this small hole in the wood" or "Take a chisel and cut a corner in this piece". In this way, the carpenter will start to get the apprentice involved in doing some small tasks. When the apprentice is doing those tasks, the carpenter will keep an eye on him/her and will give feedback, something like "Slow down, you will break the wood", or "Do not use so much pressure", or "You see the angle? This angle has to be like this" and so on. The apprentice will start to refine his/her understanding through such feedback, and gain more and more skills. Then one day the carpenter will say something like "We have too much work today. Now that you know how to do it, you can help. Create this particular piece of furniture for me on your own". The apprentice will use all the knowledge and skills learned so far in order to create what the carpenter asked for. Then the carpenter may say something like, "You are doing quite well. Carry on". That is where the fading will start.

This scenario captures the main aspects of cognitive apprenticeship. Cognitive apprenticeship starts with "world knowledge", which signifies any knowledge a person has at any point in time. Whenever we want to learn something, we always learn by making analogies. In other words, we learn by connecting new knowledge to already learnt knowledge. That is why it is important to know what a person already knows, so that connections between new knowledge and already learn knowledge can be found. Let us consider, if there is a small child who has never touched anything hot. How would we explain to that child "This is hot, don't touch it". How will you explain to a child what hot means when that child has never touched anything hot? Another hypothetical example, if there is a child who has never seen any flowers, how would you explain to that child what a garden is? Show that child a flower, then say "Now imagine you are in a place where there are lots and lots of such flowers". Just by seeing that one flower, the child can now imagine lots of flowers. Therefore, we need some initial world knowledge to learn further.

Once the initial world knowledge is identified, the next step is the observation of interactions among the experts and the peers. What it means is that just by being there and listening to other people who know what they are doing, students can start to gain some understanding by reflecting on what they see and hear. For example, students can reflect something like, "She is doing this", "He is doing that", "They are talking about it, "Why are they doing it this way?", and so on. Such simple reflections start to contribute to better understanding. Then the next step is assisting in the completion of tasks being done by the experts. In this step, the expert gives the apprentices some small task or lets them help in an ongoing task. The expert may say something like, "I am making this wooden joint", "Give me the hammer from over there", "Give me this nail", or "Give me another piece of wood". The expert is actually doing the main task, but by helping, the apprentices start to understand better and can then start to try on their own. The apprentices can try to copy how the expert did it. At that time, the expert starts to give feedback. He/she may say something like, "No, not that wood. You know, we have to create this table for outside. This wood is going to get damaged in the rain. Take that other one". Such feedback immediately provides reflection opportunities for the apprentices, in this case, to understand which particular wood is more suitable for outside and which one is not. By this stage, the apprentices start to get some theoretical knowledge and some cognitive skills.

Once the expert finds that the apprentices are progressing well, he/she can start to give new advice related to the already learnt knowledge and skills. He/she may say something like "We are using this wood here, but if we were creating a table for the seaside, we would not use this wood, because this wood cannot handle salty water". Such advice on new things from the expert is based on the progress the apprentices made during the imitation process. Depending on how the apprentices are performing, the expert can start to extend the scope of advice, including a comparison of solutions in hand with alternatives. He/she may say something like, "You are doing this now, but if you were doing for some other purpose you would need to do this differently". This type of feedback enables higher level of reflection. The apprentice may start to think something like, "I know I should use this particular thing here and not another thing, but what happens if I want to use something different?" The apprentice at this stage starts to construct new cognitive skills.

A repetition of this whole process, starting from observation, assisting, trying out, getting feedback, getting advice on new things and reflecting on it, active participation, to exploration, and innovation, enables the apprentices to achieve mastery, and they start to really work as an expert. They start to undertake new tasks on their own, start to explore new things, and even create some new ideas.

That is when the final stage of assessment comes in. The expert may say something like, "Show me how much you know?" and may give a complex task that requires integration of the various knowledge and skills learned so far, and extrapolation of those through the application of the acquired cognitive skills. If the result of that assessment is satisfactory, the expert may say "Good, now you are ready to be a carpenter on your own".

Guided discovery

Let us look at another approach, namely guided discovery, proposed by Marc Elsom-Cook in 1990, which can be used for cognitive skills acquisition (Elsom-Cook, 1990). Guided discovery starts with guided instruction. At first, some tutorial or guidance is given about the topic. Then the students observe the demonstration of various activities to understand the concepts. Then they explore those activities themselves, but this exploration and discovery part is guided. Exploration is given within limited boundaries. Only a few options are given to the students to try out, and when they do that, further guidance and feedback is given to the students. In cognitive apprenticeship there is no instruction in the first step, whereas guided discovery starts with guidance or instruction.

Learning environments for cognitive skills acquisition

So there are different models that can be used in creating adaptive and personalized learning environments and they can provide different ways for the learners to get competence. Let us look at how a cognitive apprenticeship approach can be used to create such learning environments.

Let us discuss the cognitive apprenticeship based learning environment (CABLE), which is based on a cognitive apprenticeship approach (Figure 9.1).

The CABLE provides basic domain knowledge and the application of that domain knowledge in non-contextual and contextual scenarios. What this means is that it provides general understanding of the domain and then understanding in particular situations. Once the students have observed and become familiar with different situations in which that particular domain knowledge is used, they should be able to generalize their understanding to acquire domain competence and be able to apply that knowledge in another context. So, once the student understands the knowledge in one scenario, he/she uses it in a generic sense, then in certain situations, and finally the student uses that knowledge in another context that has not yet been taught. The architecture of CABLE is based on the cognitive apprenticeship approach. Learning in the CABLE starts with observations, where the students observe how tasks are done

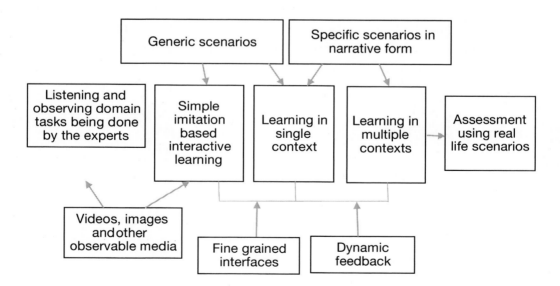

FIGURE 9.1 Main functionality of learning environments for cognitive skills acquisition

by the expert, through videos, images and other observable media. Once the students acquire basic understanding of how tasks are done, the simple imitation stage starts, where the students try to do simple tasks that they had observed. After that, advance imitation comes in where the students do more complex tasks and get feedback from the adaptivity and personalization mechanism of the CABLE. In the advance imitation stage, students try to apply the previously learned knowledge in the new context. First the CABLE shows how to apply knowledge in one particular scenario. Then the student is expected to try that in an unfamiliar scenario. If the student makes a mistake during the application of knowledge in the unfamiliar scenario, the environment asks the student to observe relevant content to understand how to do that task correctly. That is called contextual observation, where the student does not observe just anything, but that particular task where he/she made the mistake. This leads to deeper learning. The student now knows where the gaps are in his/her understanding. After that comes the interpretation of real life problems, because in real life, problems do not come as articulated statements. People have to interpret from the situation what the problem may be. They need to figure out where to even start. Learning to interpret real life problems is therefore very important. That is done in the CABLE by using narrative problems. Rather than telling "this is the problem", a case is provided, where there is a story and the student has to understand the story to find the problem. The students are expected in the CABLE to work through problems in different scenarios for repetitive training to acquire cognitive skills. Subsequently assessment is conducted to see if the student has gained competency or not.

Learning Activities

1. Select a topic of your choice and identify the conceptual knowledge, physical skills and cognitive skills related to that topic.
2. For the cognitive skills identified for the topic in the learning activity above, select what content will be suitable for observation, what activities a student should do for simple imitation, what various scenarios could provide more advance learning, and how the assessment should be conducted?

Share your ideas with your colleagues and ask them too critique. Provide feedback to your colleagues on their ideas in return.

Adaptivity and personalization in simulation based environments

Let us take another scenario of learning in which adaptivity and personalization can play an important role in providing effective learning to individual students. This scenario is based on simulation-based learning. We shall take the example of the InterSim environment (the interactive simulation based learning environment) which was created for learning about the human ear in a medical discipline (Oppermann et al., 1999). A medical discipline is typically a task-oriented discipline that requires core knowledge of medical concepts, senso-motoric skills in physical tasks (such as surgery), and cognitive skills in the diagnosis of diseases and other decision making tasks. This is in contrast with the analytical disciplines that focus primarily on domain knowledge.

The adaptivity and personalization mechanism of the InterSim learning environment enables students to explore learning content and activities in a simulation environment and provides intelligent assistance to ensure effective learning of conceptual knowledge and skills. The InterSim learning environment supports formal learning within educational institutions as well as self-learning by the students in cases where the students are not able to attend formal learning due to any constraints such as a conflict of time, the distance from educational institutions, constraints on finance resources, and others. The environment can be used in different configurations of learning, such as classroom-based learning, open and distance learning, informal learning, and learning on demand.

The target audience for InterSim learning environment is the medical students and doctors in continuing medical education, in particular those who have received their basic medical degree and are pursuing specialization in the domain of ear. For this purpose, the environment provides additional features for knowledge sharing among doctors by enabling them to add and document real cases. These cases are then also used by the InterSim environment for providing learning to the students as well as problem solving activities. The InterSim environment consists of three functional states, reflecting the three specific uses: learning, assessment and case authoring.

The learning state focuses on immediate and dynamic feedback on the students' actions with a view to facilitate active learning. The first step is to provide basic knowledge of the subject matter and overview of the domain, which is achieved with the help of tutoring and guided tours. Advanced understanding of specific areas is achieved with the help of intelligent interactive simulations. The cognitive skills are next focused by providing constructivist learning through repetitive learning. Finally, the misconceptions are identified and corrected and gaps left in earlier learning are filled with the help of domain problems. This is where notoriously difficult cases from the field, recorded by the doctors, are used by the students to attempt diagnosis and solution.

Figure 9.2 shows an example simulation interface for the diagnosis of human ear diseases. The top part of the simulation shows various parameters to select ear and parameters related to the sound, such as sound output, sound level, frequency and type of signal. There are five interrelated parts in the simulation. Part A shows the structure of the ear, along with its current state (such as fluid filled in the ear or other diseases related markings). Part B shows the audiogram. Part C shows the ear membrane (also called tympanic membrane) as seen through an otoscope, and part D shows a tympanogram. It is important to note that for a doctor, it is not possible to directly see the state of human ear. The diagnosis of the ear diseases is therefore made by analyzing and interpreting various graphs and the visualizations through an otoscope. Part E provides various parameters as measured by other instruments, for example, air pressure in the ear, fluid level, fluid viscosity and temperature, along the timeline on which the disease is progressing.

Students can manipulate any of the five parts in the simulation. Any changes in one part immediately reflect changes in other parts of the simulation. As students interact with various parts, the adaptivity and personalization mechanism monitors those interactions and provides feedback. In particular, when students go outside of acceptable values for any of the parameters, the adaptivity and personalization mechanism uses the Message Window to correct any misconceptions or gaps in the students' understanding.

The adaptivity and personalization mechanism of the InterSim learning environment provide intelligent assistance to the students through messages that are created dynamically to suit the learning situation and the current needs of the students. It provides contextually adaptive navigational aids to help students identify various interactions available with the environment. The aim for such

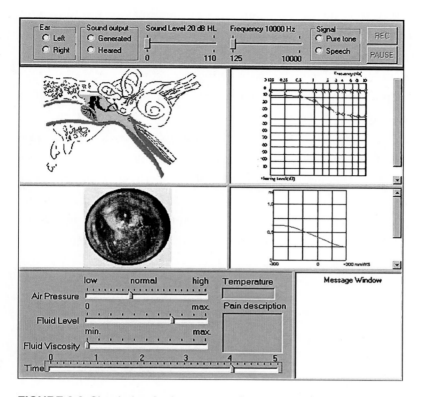

FIGURE 9.2 Simulation for human ear disease diagnosis

messages is to increase the level of useful exploration as much as possible. Subject domain related messages, on the other hand, are driven by the student interactions, and are based on the current state of student's knowledge acquisition and overall competence.

The second functional state of the InterSim learning environment focuses on assessing the knowledge and skills acquired by the students during learning state. The assessment includes measurement of both accuracy of understanding as well as the ability of applying that understanding in different contexts. This is achieved by giving students the opportunity of problem solving in different scenarios available in the real cases. The feedback in the assessment state is given to the students only after they have attempted to diagnose and solve certain medical conditions, and therefore it is of a delayed nature.

The third functional state of the InterSim learning environment enables doctors to add and document real cases in the system. Not all diseases are frequently observed by the doctors and many of them may be found only in particular geographical regions. Therefore, it is possible that the students may not encounter certain diseases too many times or perhaps at all during the whole duration of their studies. Even after completing their studies and during their initial years of practice, they may not come across some diseases. However, it is very important that even in such situations, when they do encounter any such diseases, even for the first time, they should be able to make an accurate diagnosis in order to provide appropriate treatment. That is where the real cases play important role. Doctors from any parts of the world, as and when they encounter any such rare or notoriously difficult cases, can add them to the InterSim learning environment through the functional state of case authoring. The environment then uses these cases for both learning and assessment states.

Learning Activities

1. Select a disease related to human eyes and search on the Internet for various representations and graphs that doctors use to diagnose that disease.
2. Select two or more of those representations and analyze the interrelationship between them.
3. Create a mock-up simulation to visualize those representations and describe how changes seen in one representation would affect another representation.
4. Create a list of feedback messages that the adaptivity and personalization mechanism should provide to the students when they are interacting with those representations. How would you improve students' understanding of diagnosis during those interactions using the feedback messages?

Share your ideas with your colleagues and ask them to critique. Provide feedback to your colleagues on their ideas in return.

Links

Sensory motor skills! What are they and are they even important? https://cslot.wordpress.com/2012/03/13/sensory-motor-skills-what-are-they-and-are-they-even-important/

References

Collins, A., Brown, J. S., & Newman, S. E. (1989). Cognitive apprenticeship: Teaching the crafts of reading, writing, and mathematics. In Resnick L. B. (Ed.), Knowing, learning, and instruction: essays in honor of Robert Glaser (pp. 453–494). Hillsdale, NJ: Lawrence Erlbaum Associates.

Elsom-Cook, M. T. (1990). Guided discovery tutoring: A framework for ITS research. London: Paul Chapman Publishing.

Oppermann, R., Kinshuk, Kashihara, A., Rashev, R., & Simm, H. (1999). Supporting Learner in Exploratory Learning Process in an Interactive Simulation based Learning System. Software Ergonomie '99—Design von Informationswelten (Eds. U. Arend, E. Eberleh & K. Pitschke), B. G. Teubner Stuttgart, Leipzig, 241–253 (ISBN 3-519-02694-5).

ten

Reusability in Adaptive and Personalization Learning

To provide appropriate support to the students, adaptive and personalized learning environments select different learning contents, customize the presentation of that content, and select appropriate navigational approaches, to suit specific needs of a student at a certain time. A variety of learning content is therefore needed for each concept covered in the subject matter, preferably in different formats, so that the adaptivity and personalization mechanism can select appropriate content. This approach puts additional demands for creating vast amount of learning content on the teachers, who are already overloaded. This situation has given rise to the need for sharing and reusing learning content among teachers, particularly for those subjects that are commonly taught at many institutions. In this chapter, we shall look at the concept of reusability. We shall discuss how teachers can find learning contents created by other teachers, how they can make their own learning content available to others, and how reusability can go beyond sharing of learning content to learning activities and even learning scenarios.

Learning objects

When teachers create any learning content, they typically create some sort of multimedia object. It may be an image, a video, an animation, or some other object. Once they create the object, they know its purpose, where they want to use it, for what course and topic this object is suitable for, whether it is for watching or doing some hands-on activity, and whether it is targeted for some particular students. So they do not have to make any documentation to be able to use it. However, if they want to share that object with other teachers, they will need to make all this information available, so that others can check whether that object fits their needs. Even more, for a teacher to be able to search for useful objects created by others, this information needs to be in some consistent form, so that others can select certain parameters and search for specific requirements. This standard format of information is called metadata, and the multimedia object with accompanied metadata is called learning object. This metadata can either be embedded within the object (for example, as meta-tags in HTML) or held separately in a database, also known as a metadata repository.

Learning objects, because of their accompanied metadata in standardized form, can be used and reused in different contexts, once they are created. They can also be assembled together in different ways to create different types of learning content. For example, the same learning object can be used by a teacher as part of a learning unit, while other teacher may use it as part of an exercise, example or even a quiz. Learning objects provide excellent opportunity for adaptive and personalized learning environments to automatically select appropriate content to suit the requirements of individual students in real time. Examples of learning objects include video demonstrations, tutorials, stories, simulations, and so on. Even more complex learning objects can be created by combining smaller learning objects. For example, learning objects can represent case studies that have been created by combining many other learning objects.

Learning object repositories

For a learning object to be useful for a wider academic community, it needs to be reusable, so that it can be used in different contexts. It needs to be interoperable so that it can be used in different environments, platforms and computers. It also needs to be accessible, so that others can find it through some sort of search mechanism. A number of learning object repositories have emerged over the years with the aim to manage learning objects and the associated metadata. Some of these are generic and contain all sorts of learning objects whereas others have been built to serve some specific communities. To satisfy different aims and requirements, different metadata schemas have emerged to describe learning objects. Adaptive and personalized learning environments therefore need to not only search among a large number of different repositories but also to deal with different metadata schemas. Two of these schemas have been approved by recognized standards organizations or by industry as de-facto standards. These include the Learning Technology Standards Committee of the Institution of Electrical and Electronics Engineers (IEEE) and the Subcommittee 36 of the International Organization for Standardization's (ISO) Joint Technical Committee 1. There are also metadata schema specifications that are not as evolved as standards but they capture a rough consensus within the community, for example, Dublin Core Metadata Initiative. Based on the standards and specifications, application profiles have been developed to serve the needs of a particular community of users, such as CanCore, which is an application of IEEE Learning Object Metadata, and EdNa, which is an application of Dublin Core.

With all these standards, specifications and application profiles serving different communities, it becomes important to find a way for adaptive and personalized learning environments to communicate with the repositories effectively be able to work with them. However, it is very difficult if not impossible for one learning environment to support all various standards, specifications and application profiles. One possible solution to this problem is to have a conversion mechanism from one schema to another, so that different systems can use that mechanism when they need learning objects from a repository that uses a different type of metadata. Yuejun Zhang and colleagues suggested an example of such a conversion mechanism (Zhang et al. 2005).

Content packaging

Learning objects are used by the learning environments to create learning units, learning activities, and other components used in the learning process. To be able to reuse these different components among different learning environments, standards have also been created to share content packages. One example is Advanced Distributed Learning's Sharable Content Object Reference Model (SCORM), which is a collection of standards and specifications that enable sequencing of learning objects using a set of rules to specify the order in which a student is expected to experience learning objects. IMS Global Learning Consortium provided the content packaging format, using an Extensible Markup Language (XML) manifest file wrapped up inside a zip file containing the learning content. This format was then used by SCORM.

To capture learning activities in the learning environment, which are used by different people who use different pedagogical strategies and may have different learning goals, IMS Global Learning Consortium developed IMS Learning Design (LD), which is a specification to describe these pedagogical strategies and learning goals, with an aim to share them between different learning environments. IMS Learning Design describe the different roles people can play, which work towards certain learning objectives, in order to complete different learning activities in a learning environment. IMS Learning Design is particularly relevant for the adaptive and personalized learning environments, as it supports customization of learning experience by enabling conditions in which certain content is presented to the students, using DIV layers to customize certain part of learning content, and make visible certain content in certain situations.

Test your understanding

1. What is the difference between a multimedia object and a learning object?
2. What are the different ways in which metadata can be stored for a learning object?
3. What is the difference between standard, specification and application profile?
4. Why IMS Learning Design is relevant for adaptivity and personalization?

Reflection

- Is reusability useful for all teachers or only a particular group of teachers? Justify your response with examples.

Reusability in the learning process analysis

Another aspect of reusability that has emerged in recent years is in the analysis of learning process. To be able to provide effective support to individual students, the adaptive and personalized learning environments need to analyze different types of information about the student, the environment in which the student is learning, and the instructional scenario in which the student is engaged. This information comes from variety of sources. For example, the student's personal data may be stored in student management systems, information about the student's competence may come from the learning management system, information about the student's environment may be received from the sensors of the student's mobile phone, and so on. Adaptive and personalized learning environments analyze this diverse and heterogeneous information through a process called Learning Analytics, which looks for various patterns in the learning process of individual students, a group of students and a whole cohort of students over different periods of time, to understand what works for certain types of students and what not, what kind of content is suitable for students with certain learning styles, which areas of instructions are working well and which may need revision, and so on. These environments then need to make sense out of this process to be able to provide meaningful information to different people, such as students, teachers, principals, and so on, according to their individual requirements. For example, students need to be provided with information about how they are progressing in the leaning process, and perhaps where they stand among the rest of the students in their class, whereas teachers would need to have information about different students in their courses, whether groups of students doing a project are progressing or not, whether there are any parts of learning content that the majority of students have problems understanding, and so on.

The learning analytics process within the adaptive and personalized learning environments therefore need to understand information coming out of various other sources, analyse it, and provide appropriate visualizations to different people to satisfy their requirements. They also need to be able to provide the analysis to other environments in order for those environments to use it. Similarly, they may need the analysis information from other environments in a format that they themselves can understand. That is where learning analytics specifications play a significant role. One example of such a specification, which is moving towards becoming standard is Caliper, proposed by IMS Global Learning Consortium. Caliper provides a mechanism to consistently capture and present measures of learning activities, so that learning analytics features can be developed and implemented more efficiently in learning environments. It provides a common language for tagging the data related to the learning process, so that different learning environments can use it and share it with common understanding. It is built with a view to offer more meaning and context to each learning related data and to integrate disparate analysis and measurements from a vast range of tools and environments. It enables learning environments to observe or sense, store, analyze, reflect on, give feedback, visualize and provide regulation in consistent and standardized manner.

Caliper is built on top of and by extending various other specifications. Let us look at some of the examples:

Learning Tools Interoperability (LTI) Standard: It allows seamless connectivity between different web-based, externally hosted applications and content, and tools such as chat applications and more sophisticated learning environments, and platforms that use them for interaction with the students. LTI enables developers to use programming language of their own choice to write the integration mechanism. Learning environments do not need to be updated every time a new application needs to be added to the environment. All different tools and applications work with each other without requiring students to log in separately in each of them. LTI also allows teachers to link to new applications with instant access, so they can use them with ease in their courses immediately.

Question & Test Interoperability (QTI) Standard: It provides a standard way to represent questions and tests, and associated results. It facilitates exchange of these items between various authoring tools, item banks, test creation tools, learning environments, and assessment delivery systems.

Accessible Portable Item Protocol (APIP) Standard: It provides a mechanism to standardize the format of data interchange for digital test items, which can be used by the assessment programs and the developers of question items. The basic purpose of APIP is to facilitate exchange of question items and tests. It is based on QTI and also supports LTI.

Common Cartridge (CC): It describes format for creation and sharing of digital learning content. It provides a standard method for representing digital course material to be used in a wide variety of learning environments. It also allows for modular, web-based, interactive and customizable publishing of digital content in online courses.

Learning Information Services (LIS) Standard: It defines how learning environments manage the exchange of information that describes people, groups, memberships, courses and outcomes within learning context.

Content Packaging (CP): It enables the exchange of data in a standard format between different learning environments that would like to import, export, aggregate, and disaggregate packages of learning content. For example, it enables the export of learning content from one learning environment and importing that exported content into another learning environment without losing information that describes the media in the content package and the structure information, such as table of contents.

In learning environments, the learning curriculum is generally composed and delivered as a collection or sequence of one or more learning activities. Different learning activities can be grouped into one or more types, such as quizzes, lectures, reading, projects, assessment, collaboration, and so on. Caliper uses IMS Learning Metric Profiles, which are created for each of these types and define a standardized, structured collection of learning activity metrics to represent granular measurements specific to actions of students within each type of activity. For example, various actions with reading type include making annotations, using pages or blocks, using media and lookups. Various actions in quiz type include scores of students, number of attempts, remediations, and associated references. The type of gaming includes actions of progress, cognition, attempts, hints and collaboration. The Learning Activity Metric Profiles work closely with the IMS Sensor API, which supports the instrumentation, collection and exchange of data from various learning tools and environments, and associated learning content elements.

The Sensor API supports the exchange of learning events based on interactions with or on learning activities. These learning events are expressed in the form of a data triple—"LearningContext"—"Action"—"ActivityContext". This is similar to the RDF Triple form "subject/predicate/object" used by World Wide Web Consortium. The learning events allow for the expression of the measurement of an interaction with a learning activity.

Test your understanding

1. Explain the purpose of Learning Analytics.
2. What is Learning Tools Interoperability Standard?
3. How does Content Packaging help in reusability of learning content?
4. What is the role of IMS Sensor API?

Reusable learning scenarios

We have looked at reusability of learning content, activities, and analysis of learning process within the adaptive and personalized learning environments. With more and more mobile devices with built-in different sensors, it is now possible for these environments to extend their support for the students away from computer screens and provide a customization of the learning process in ubiquitous environments where students can use physical objects with online information to learn in authentic settings. Learning in such settings requires the learning environments to customize the learning process to the context of a particular location, and create unique learning activities that can use the resources available in that particular location and suit the conditions of the situation of that location. For example, if there is a particular painting available in a particular art gallery, then a learning activity related to that painting can only be done in that art gallery. At the same time, the learning environment needs to ensure that the learning activity is possible within the constraints of that art gallery. Creation of learning activities in various geographical locations, in various situations, is not a trivial task for a teacher who may not be physically present at the time a student has the possibility to learn at that location. Therefore reuse of learning scenarios in such ubiquitous learning environments becomes an important issue.

Let us look at an example of how learning scenarios can be created in ubiquitous learning environments that can be reused by different students.

To support reuse of learning scenarios in ubiquitous learning environments, a methodology has been developed to create IMS Content Packages and IMS Learning Design in authentic learning context. Authoring is ubiquitous environments takes advantage of opportunistic learning, where the student happens to be at a place where the adaptive and personalized learning environment detects possibility to provide learning to support the student's learning goal. In such situations, learning is not pre-planned, leading to two possible options. There may be an example scenario available that was created by either a teacher or by a student who was in that location at some earlier time. If the example scenario was created by a student, a teacher would need to authenticate it before it can be used by the learning environment for other students. The second option is that the learning environment finds various resources that are available in that location that can help the student in the learning process, but there is no previously created example scenario available. In that case, the learning environment can present the opportunity to that student for creating and recording an example scenario, which can then be assessed and authenticated by a teacher and made available for other students.

Use of mobile sensors, such as camera, microphone, GPS and accelerometer allow for tracking physical surroundings, location and a student's movement without obstructing his/her learning activities. However, all this data from different sensors comes in different formats and it is difficult to make any meaningful inferences without converting it into a structured form and tagging it with metadata. Creation of standard metadata in a ubiquitous environment in real time when an example scenario is being created also requires a solution that can be used through mobile devices. Mobile Authentic Authoring in IMS (MAAIMS) is one such solution that captures learning scenarios in authentic settings using mobile devices, which can then be enriched with location coordinates and other descriptive metadata, using IMS metadata specifications (Kinshuk and Jesse, 2013). Use of IMS Content Packages and IMS Learning Design makes it possible for the scenario to be shared with learning environments other than the one which facilitated the creation.

MAAIMS is a ubiquitous application, part of which runs on mobile phones that have certain sensors to capture the data related to the learning scenario and another part resides on a web server, where computations take place and data is stored. The mobile device component connects to the server component through Internet. When a student accepts the invitation of the adaptive and personalized learning environment to create a learning scenario, MAAIMS application is opened on the student's mobile device, and a new learning scenario is initiated. At this point, MAAIMS queries the location of the scenario. This ensures that each scenario is properly geo-tagged before the student has possibility to move from that location. However, the student must explicitly agree to record the location information. This way, the student can select to tag location to only those scenarios that are truly location dependent. The MAAIMS application then asks for initial learning object metadata such as title, keywords, and so on. Once the initial metadata has been entered, the student is given option to capture various multimedia components of the scenario, for example, audio, video, images, and so on. Depending on the option selected by the student, the application launches respective recording application, such as audio recorder, camera or video recorder. The student can then capture the learning scenario using a combination of multimedia objects. The MAAIMS application also allows the captured learning scenario to be played, so that the quality of recording can be ascertained, and if needed, discarded and recaptured before requiring metadata tagging.

After the student has captured the learning scenario and entered the required metadata, the application then presents the student with an option to add Learning Design, which enables the student to create a learning activity attached to the learning scenario. Then the whole package of learning scenario, metadata, location information and learning activity is uploaded to the server component for the teacher's assessment and authentication. Once the learning scenario has been authenticated by the teacher, it becomes available for other students.

When another student goes near the location where a particular learning scenario was captured, he/she is alerted by the MAAIMS application regarding the existence of the scenario. The student can then watch the multimedia objects related to that scenario to gain the understanding. At that moment, if there is also a learning activity attached to that scenario, the application offers the student to undertake that activity. If the student agrees to do that activity, the adaptive and personalized environment takes over and guides the student in the learning process. The student can then choose to create his/her own learning scenario with different perspective, and can use the MAAIMS application to record and store it for future use by others.

Learning activities

1. Select a topic in a subject of your choice.
2. Identify a physical object that can be used to create a learning activity for the topic you selected.
3. Identify what online information may be useful to interact with that physical object.
4. Create a learning activity scenario that uses the physical object and online information.
5. Select what multimedia format(s) would be suitable to record that learning activity.

Share your findings with your colleagues and ask for their critique. Provide your critique on their findings in return.

Links

IMS Caliper Analytics: www.imsglobal.org/activity/caliperram

IMS Learning Design: www.imsglobal.org/learningdesign/index.html

Learning object metadata: https://en.wikipedia.org/wiki/Learning_object_metadata

Learning object repository: http://edutechwiki.unige.ch/en/Learning_object_repository, also see http://edutechwiki.unige.ch/en/Learning_objects_repositories for a list of various repositories

IEEE Standard for Learning Object Metadata: http://standards.ieee.org/findstds/standard/1484.12.1-2002.html

Resources

CanCore: http://cancore.athabascau.ca/en/

Dublin Core: http://dublincore.org/

EdNa: http://edna.wikispaces.com/EdNA+Metadata+Standard+1.1

Institution of Electrical and Electronics Engineers Learning Technology Standards Committee: http://ieee-sa.centraldesktop.com/ltsc/

International Organization for Standardization's Joint Technical Committee 1 Subcommittee 36: www.iso.org/iso/home/standards_development/list_of_iso_technical_committees/iso_technical_committee.htm?commid=45392

References

Kinshuk, & Jesse, R. (2013). Reusable Authentic Learning Scenario Creation in Ubiquitous Learning Environments. In Huang, R., Kinshuk, & Spector, J. M. (Eds.), *Reshaping Learning—Frontiers of Learning Technology in a Global Context*, Heidelberg: Springer, 273–298.

Zhang Y., Kinshuk, & Lin T. (2005). An Open-ended Framework for Learning Object Metadata Interchange. In Looi C.-K., Jonassen D. & Ikeda M. (Eds.), *Towards Sustainable and Scalable Educational Innovations Informed by the Learning Sciences*, Amsterdam: IOS Press, 950–953.

part four

VALIDATION AND
FUTURE TRENDS

eleven
Evaluation of Adaptive and Personalized Systems

Adaptive and personalized learning environments have come a long way since their introduction a couple of decades ago. Research in this area has matured to a level that commercial implementations have started to emerge. To promote their wider use, careful and systematic scrutiny of these environments becomes an important issue. While there are a number of evaluation methods available, there is no single method that can effectively validate an adaptive and personalized learning environment as a whole. Different evaluation methods serve different purpose. Some evaluate certain system functionality while others look at certain aspect of the environment. Some methods are useful at early formative stages when the environment is still in design and development stage whereas others are geared for the time of its use. Given the variety and diversity of these methods, it is not easy for educators to identify which methods are appropriate in their context. Therefore understanding of these different methods is crucial to be able to select appropriate method for the intended purpose.

Evaluation principles

Evaluation of adaptive and personalized learning environment is still an area that is not matured. Most of the researchers working in the area of adaptive and personalized learning have focused primarily on the potential of such environments and with the implementation of the functionality, and have not paid much attention to verifying whether the environments are indeed efficient and effective. That is perhaps one reason why the commercial world has not been able to see the value of these environments, resulting in very little uptake for wider implementations.

Let us first discuss various reasons why evaluation of adaptive and personalized learning environments is important, before looking at various methods of evaluation that can be used for this purpose. This discussion is particularly important because evaluation of adaptive and personalized learning environments is a costly and time consuming task, particularly because the evaluation of the effectiveness and efficiency of adaptivity and personalization on learning process is not a trivial process. However, if done properly it enables the teachers to understand two major aspects: the pedagogical benefits of the environment on the learning process, and the link between the functionality of the environment with its actual behavior that the students experience. Evaluation also helps in understanding better about each component of the environment and gradually improving them over time, as the results of further evaluation show whether the changes made due to previous evaluation feedback resulted in improvement of the functionality or vice-versa. This process of continuous evaluation-improvement-evaluation has potential to not only improve the usability of the adaptive and personalized learning environment but also affecting positively its lifespan.

Different evaluation methods consider different factors, which makes it difficult to generalize the results of evaluation and to compare different environments that have been evaluated by using different evaluation methods. It is also important to note that the majority of evaluation methods used nowadays to evaluate adaptive and personalized learning environments were not devised for this purpose. Their origins differ and many of them have been adapted from other areas such as education, psychology and computer science. The main issues at heart for evaluating adaptive and personalized learning environments center around two questions: i) How does the adaptive and personalized learning environment affect the learning process of students for a given subject domain? ii) Does each functionality of the adaptive and personalized learning environment result in the intended behavior of the environment?

Evaluation process also helps in the overall thinking process of the developers of the environment, as it focuses on critical issues of appropriateness, usability and quality in system design, instead of only looking for somehow delivering the system as quickly as possible. However, ad-hoc evaluation processes typically used for evaluating adaptive and personalized learning environments do not lead to any long-term benefits, since they neither pinpoint chronic problems nor do they enable sharing of experiences in order to avoid common mistakes. Consequently, there is a need for a more systematic approach to evaluation.

Reflection

1. Why is it important to evaluate adaptive and personalized learning environments when the process could be costly and time consuming?
2. What problems may arise if an adaptive and personalized learning environment is implemented and used with students without evaluating it?

Perspectives of evaluation

A number of evaluations methods are available that can be used to evaluate adaptive and personalized learning environments. To make some sense and order among these methods, we shall look at them from two perspectives.

The first perspective focuses on the views expressed by David Littman and Elliot Soloway regarding the degree of evaluation, where they identified internal evaluation, which covers evaluation methods to test a component of a system, and external evaluation, which encompasses methods that evaluate whole system (Littman and Soloway, 1988). The second perspective focuses on the suitability of individual evaluation method in a particular context. It looks at how findings of a particular application of an evaluation method in an experimental condition relate to all the evidence available through exploratory research about the performance of a particular component of functionality of the environment. While the experimental process of evaluation identifies the effect of independent variables on dependent variables and requires statistically significant results from randomly assigned group of participants, the exploration process involves analysis of the environment in real use where the number of users may not be consistent and data may not be precise.

Let us now look at different evaluation methods that can be used to evaluate adaptive and personalized learning environments.

Test your understanding

1. What is the difference between internal evaluation and external evaluation methods?

Evaluation methods for adaptive and personalized learning environments

We shall first discuss those evaluation methods that are more suitable for an experimental approach. These evaluation methods focus on the impact of independent variables on dependent variables within a specified and controlled experimental setting. A systematic methodology is required for these methods with random assignment of participants and statistically significant outcomes.

- *Proof of correctness:* This evaluation method evaluates individual components of the environment. It uses hypothesis testing approach in experimental settings and is suitable for internal evaluation. The purpose of this evaluation method is to verify whether the functionality of each component of the environment matches with the structure and specifications of that component, and whether that component contributes towards the overall requirements and goals of the environment.
- *Additive experimental design:* This evaluation method is particularly suitable for evaluating impact of individual components of adaptive and personalized learning environments. It allows for modifying the various

variables in experimental settings, and therefore suits primarily to internal experiment-based evaluations. The method requires a large number of participants and therefore only cost effective if the component being evaluated is sufficiently large. One benefit of this method is that it allows for manipulation of individual aspects of the environment so that they can be directly evaluated for their impact on the overall environment functionality.

- *Diagnostic accuracy:* This evaluation method is suitable for internal evaluation of the adaptive and personalized learning environments, as it allows for validating the accuracy of recognition and interpretation of errors made by the students in order to provide subsequent pedagogical support. It also enables assessment of the quality of the pedagogical and instructional design principles used in the environment. This method is suitable for assessing internal functionality of the pedagogical component of the adaptive and personalized learning environments under controlled experimental conditions.

- *Feedback/instruction quality:* This evaluation method validates the impact of feedback of adaptivity and personalization mechanism and the instructional quality of the environment on the learning process through experimental settings. It uses lag sequential analysis procedures and therefore is suitable for internal evaluation. This is typically done by calculating lag sequential probability, which is the ratio of actions in a specific category to the total number of actions that occur within a specific frame following a target action. This method allows for validating different levels of details of the feedback given to the student by the adaptivity and personalization mechanism as well as different types of feedback.

- *Sensitivity analysis:* This method allows inspection of different responses resulting from providing varying information to the individual components of the adaptive and personalized learning environments or the whole environment itself in experimental settings. It is therefore suitable for both internal and external evaluations. This method is particularly suitable to verify the accuracy of individualized instructional support by varying the student parameters and checking the effect on the environment's response.

- *Experimental research:* This evaluation method evaluates the relationship between a set of interventions and the outcome. Therefore, it is well suited to examine the effects of the teaching pedagogy used in the adaptive and personalized learning environments. A number of research designs can be used within this method, including single group designs, control group designs, and quasi-experimental designs. This evaluation method provides feedback on the overall effectiveness of the environment and therefore more appropriate for external evaluation.

- *Product evaluation:* This evaluation method can be used to evaluate overall effectiveness and efficiency of the adaptive and personalized learning environments. The purpose of this evaluation method is to determine whether the development of a particular environment should be continued. It enables comparison of instructional effectiveness of the adaptive and personalized learning environments, human teachers and traditional methods of instruction by analyzing the performance data. It is primarily suitable for environments that have large number of students. Due to its classical nature of comparing different learning conditions, this method uses experimental approach of evaluation.

The next category of evaluation methods explores real implementations of the adaptive and personalized learning environments in great detail when the students are actually learning in the environment. All sorts of data available during the learning process from different sources are analyzed. In such evaluation methods, the number of participants is usually small and evaluation method is not very precise.

- *Expert inspection:* This method evaluates whether an adaptive and personalized learning environment is meeting the desired level of performance. It is useful for evaluating individual components of the environment and therefore suitable for internal evaluations. Since this methods does not test any hypothesis, it is considered as an exploratory method instead of experimental method.
- *Level of agreement:* This method looks for correlation of level of agreement between different subject matter experts for verification of the learning content in the adaptive and personalized learning environment. It is therefore suitable for internal evaluation. It attempts to estimate the consistency belief among experts regarding the learning content, and therefore is an exploratory method.

- *Wizard of Oz:* In this method, a human simulates the behavior of the proposed adaptive and personalized learning environment, and therefore allows for testing various aspects of the design of the environment before implementation. It can therefore be considered as internal evaluation. Since it is difficult to predict in advance how the human simulating the behavior will behave, it is not possible to identify which parameters to observe and how. Therefore this evaluation method is exploratory by nature.

- *Performance metrics:* This method explores individual characteristics and functionality of an adaptive and personalized learning environment using quantitative methods. It is therefore suitable for internal evaluation. This method is particularly suited in situations where number of participants is too small to arrive to any statistically significant results, and hence it is more of an exploratory nature. Particular usage of this method includes assessment of various components of the environment by analyzing the accuracy of feedback to the students, how students use various features of the environment, and the changes among students over a time period.

- *Internal evaluation:* This evaluation method is suitable for detailed exploration of the architecture of the adaptive and personalized learning environment and its intended behavior. This is typically done by looking at the code, intended result of that code and actual outcome of that code. This method can be used to evaluate the learning content and pedagogy used in the environment, the adaptivity and personalization algorithms, and system performance by analyzing how the functionality of various components of the environment compares with simpler versions of those components.

- *Criterion-based evaluation:* This evaluation method enables exploration of the inadequacies of the adaptive and personalized learning environment by drawing up the requirements and specifications in the form of a checklist. Since this method can be used for both the components of the environment and the whole environment itself, it is suitable for both internal and external evaluations.

- *Pilot testing:* This method evaluates the design of the adaptive and personalized learning environment for any unexpected outcomes while the environment is being used by the students. It is essentially exploratory in nature and is useful for identifying problems in the intended functionality of the environment. This method can be used to test individual components as well as whole environment. It can be used for testing the environment with a single student in early stages of development, in small group setting when the majority of the functionality has been developed, and large scale pilots when the development of the environment has been completed.

- *Certification:* This method is based on similar methods applied to certify the competence of human teachers. It is exploratory in nature and enables authoritative endorsement of the accuracy of the functionality of the adaptive and personalized learning environment. Since this method looks at the suitability of whole environment, it is suitable for external evaluation.

- *Outside assessment:* This method looks at the level of agreement of the opinions of experts and/or large number of students who are either using or potentially use the adaptive and personalized learning environment. This method can be conducted by either inviting the experts to observe and evaluate the functionality of the environment or remotely asking questions to a selected group of experts. It relies upon the exploration of the opinions, and therefore exploratory and external in nature.

- *Existence proofs:* This method analyzes the success of the implementation of the adaptive and personalized learning environment. Since it relates to whole environment, it is suitable for external evaluation. Application of this method requires clear description of the goals and assumptions of the evaluation, discussion on design decisions, and documentation of the findings in terms of what worked and what not. It is therefore exploratory in nature.

- *Observation and qualitative classification of phenomena:* This method aims to identify classes of phenomena, patterns, and trends in the way students and teachers interact with the adaptive and personalized learning environments. It is exploratory in nature as it primarily uses observation data either in real or contrived situations.

- *Structured tasks and quantitative classification of phenomena:* This method uses structured approaches to collect responses of students and teachers, by using external evaluation approaches, such as interviews, questionnaires and surveys. This method generally results in a large amount of structured and precise data.

- *Comparison studies:* This evaluation method records the similarities and differences between the behavior and/or design of an adaptive and personalized learning environment with another environment. Since this method looks at overall performance of the environment, it is essentially exploratory in nature and is suitable for external evaluation. It can compare the environment by assessing the performance against another well-known environment, by making abstract comparisons of generalizability and extendibility of the approach used by the environment with other environments, and by simulating the behavior of another environment.

Test your understanding

1. In what situations an experimental evaluation approach is useful?
2. Give an example of evaluation method that is external and exploratory in nature.

Some considerations for evaluation of the adaptive and personalized learning environments

Let us look at some practical issues that should be considered while evaluating the adaptive and personalized learning environments. Since adaptive and personalized learning environments are still mostly in research stage and have not gained widespread implementation, the evaluation process needs to start by analyzing the limitations of the currently available adaptive and personalized learning environments. For example, the majority of the environments typically consider only a few needs and characteristics of students and therefore provide limited adaptivity and personalization support during learning process. They are developed for either specific subject domain or offer specific features that do not cover adaptive support for the complete learning process. The majority of these environments primarily focus on the students and do not provide comprehensive features for teachers to enable them to intervene in the learning process. There is a lack of standardization in these environments, which means that the teachers get trapped in a particular environment and cannot reuse the content and activities they have created in one environment to another environment. This makes migration from one environment to another impossible, and leads to reluctance by the teachers in using any environment.

Therefore, the first issue that the evaluation of the adaptive and personalized learning environments needs to consider is the ways in which the individual characteristics and needs of the students can be accommodated in the environment with an aim to improve the learning experience. The evaluation process can study this issue by looking at how the environment accommodates different learning styles, cognitive abilities and affective states of the students. Exploratory evaluation can be conducted to study how the students with different characteristics behave in such environments, how these environments can reliably identify characteristics of individual students, and how they can provide adequate adaptive and personalized support to students with different characteristics.

Taking learning styles as an example, the first question the evaluation needs to cover is whether learning styles are stable over time, and then analyze how learning styles can be measured considering there are a lot of different learning style models available in the literature. Even further, the evaluation also needs to establish whether students actually prefer different ways of learning, and what happens when students encounter courses where the course structure and content matches or does not match with an individual student's learning style. The next step in the evaluation process would be to look at the ways in which the environment provides adaptivity and personalization support for different learning styles and analyze each and every aspects of that support for measuring efficiency and effectiveness, and identifying any inadequacies.

The next issue in an evaluation of the adaptive and personalized learning environments is to explore additional ways in which data can be collected to improve the adaptivity and personalization support. Continuing with the example of learning styles, this can lead to the analysis of the impact the strength of a student's learning style preference may have on student's performance. The evaluation can also consider which learning styles have more impact on an individual student's performance, and how students with different learning styles and different achievements behave in a course where adaptivity and personalization mechanism does not align the course content and presentation to the student's preferred learning styles. The evaluation can explore the strategies students use in such situation to see whether these strategies give any indications about students' achievements and whether adaptivity and personalization mechanism could learn from these strategies to provide better support to the students.

A representative scenario

Let us now look at an example of evaluation on a fully operational adaptive and personalized learning environment. This environment has been aimed at students learning the knowledge and skills in the marginal costing subject in cost engineering/accounting domain. The purpose of the evaluation is to assess the value and effectiveness of the environment for the students.

The evaluation method is selected to first compare the environment with traditional instructional approaches, and then to determine the features that are significant for evaluating an adaptive and personalized learning environment. Two evaluation requirements are identified:

(i)   Should the whole environment be evaluated or only certain functionality?
(ii) Is an experimental approach possible given the number of students using the environment and other environmental conditions?

Since the aim of this evaluation is to assess the value and effectiveness of the whole environment, the evaluation is narrowed down to an external evaluation. The second question needs deeper analysis. Since the comparison of the environment with traditional instructional approaches require hypothesis testing to identify which approach is better, an experimental evaluation method seems the right choice. However, this also requires collection of opinions of the students using the environment as well as those going through traditional classroom based instruction, which leads to an exploratory approach. As a compromise, the decision is made to select two evaluation methods, one for experimental study and another for exploratory research. As identified earlier, both methods must suit to external evaluation. Therefore, *structured tasks and quantitative classification of phenomena* method is selected where a structured questionnaire is used as the instrument for collecting the opinions of the students. Subsequently, product evaluation method is used to analyze the differences between the instructional method used by the adaptive and personalized learning environment and that used in the traditional approach. This is achieved by a before-after two-group experiment.

Learning activity

1. Create a list of questions that an evaluation process should consider for analyzing the support for student motivation by an adaptive and personalized learning environment. Share your thoughts with your colleagues and ask for their critique. Provide critique on their thoughts in return.

References

Littman, D., & Soloway, E. (1988). Evaluating ITSs: The cognitive science perspective. In Polson M. C. & Richardson J. J. (Eds.), *Foundations of Intelligent Tutoring Systems*, New Jersey: Lawrence Erlbaum, 209–242.

twelve
Future Development and Research Issues

Adaptive and personalized learning environments have come a long way. In the early nineties, the evolution of web-based learning provided tremendous opportunities for educators and students but also created a number of challenges: How to support students while exploring content on the Internet during the learning process? How to customize learning content and activities to suit the demands of pedagogy in an environment which is not directly controlled by the teacher? How to customize the learning process for students with different characteristics as they access the learning environment from different parts of the world?

Mobile learning and ubiquitous learning

The explosion of mobile devices has created further expectations in terms of mobile learning. While mobile devices allow students to learn outside of a classroom, in authentic environments, using real problems, providing support during learning process in real time is a challenge. Assessment processes also need reconsideration to align them with the new ways of learning that mobile devices afford. Old ways of assessing students to write a two-hour exam in an examination room does not lend itself to assess the knowledge and skills learned in hands-on authentic learning environments. Another challenge is to support learning anytime and anywhere while tackling with the limitations of mobile devices, their heterogeneity, and their evolution.

Mobile learning has further evolved into ubiquitous learning, where students engage with both physical objects and electronic information in authentic environments to undertake hands-on activities. These learning anytime and anywhere situations pose a number of issues: How to contextualize learning to students' situational, spatial and temporal context? How to foster authentic learning by infusing physical objects with virtual information? How to make assessment of ubiquitous learning relevant to learning process itself?

The role of teacher in ubiquitous learning also needs further clarity: How can teachers support learning process effectively in an environment where learning process is dictated by the context of the students and their surroundings? What pedagogy shifts are in order to support learning in ubiquitous environments?

Let us take an example of this new paradigm shift, facilitated by ubiquitous learning. A group of primary school children in a Canadian city are visiting a zoo. The ubiquitous-learning-based adaptive and personalized learning environment detects the location of the kids through their mobile devices and identifies that they are currently looking at bison. The adaptivity and personalization mechanism of the environment can then give the kids some interesting facts about the bison and can also tell them that the bison they are looking at are one of many kinds of bison that exist in different parts of the world. It can show them photos of the different kinds of bison and can also give some information on the main differences between various kinds. The mechanism can go to the next step—it can try to find if there is any other group of children in another part of the world who happen to be looking at bison in their own city. If it finds one, it can ask the Canadian kids if they would like to talk to that other group to discuss what they are looking at, how the bison in two places are different, and so on. The technological advances now allow such learning in authentic environments, where learning activities can use both physical objects and electronic information in real-time.

Ubiquitous learning allows for taking learning outside of the classroom. For example, science experiments can be conducted in real physical environments—say, teachers can look at the properties of a plant in a garden and record the video of that activity. The video is then stored in the media repository of the ubiquitous learning environment. Then the adaptivity and personalization mechanism of the ubiquitous learning environment can prompt a student who is in that location and can benefit from that video. Once the student has watched the video, the environment can suggest that the student undertake that activity. And can guide the student during that activity by providing supporting explanations.

Ubiquitous-learning-based adaptive and personalized learning environments focus on individual strengths and needs of the individual students. They allow various types of learning scenarios, both in class and outdoor situations, in order to enable learning in the students' personal contexts. This can improve the relevance of the learning scenarios to the students' living and work environments, resulting in better understanding and better learning experience.

By integrating physical as well as virtual resources, ubiquitous-learning-based adaptive and personalized learning environments can also make extensive use of open education resources, enabling teachers and students to tap into the vast resources available on the Internet.

A ubiquitous learning approach aligns well with the changing learning needs of today's students. It provides a means to shift away from older models of educational delivery that were defined by having the teacher and students in the same room. Students today have demanding schedules, requiring flexibility in terms of time and location of learning. They prefer individualized learning opportunities. They have access to a vast amount of digital resources accessible through their mobile devices, so they are less reliant on the content provided by the teachers. They have the Internet at their fingertips. They have the possibility to learn wherever they are. If they do not understand something, right there they can open up an Internet browser on their mobile device and search for it while looking at a physical object. They also have increased accessibility of physical resources within their own living and work environment that can be used for learning purposes, as these resources can be identified and found using location, camera and other sensors on their mobile devices.

These changing learning needs of the students are also affecting the instructional requirements. The old models of physical proximity of teachers with students for observation and evaluation do not work anymore. Additionally, the kind of exposure to open resources and different learning choices that students have, that is also making it difficult for teachers to physically observe the student and predict their behaviour in terms of what kind of learning resources students will select.

At the same time the amount of data that is becoming available about students' learning process is getting bigger and bigger. Students generate countless interactions as they move from one location to another to undertake learning activities, they take pictures, they take videos, they search for some keywords on their mobile devices, they log into the learning management system, they go from one unit to another in the system, they take quizzes, they do different assignments, they click here, they click there, and they talk to someone using an online communication tool. There are lots of different ways the data is being generated both from interaction with physical objects and from accessing online systems. With all this data coming in from different students, the challenge is to analyze it effectively to make sense of it and to use it to provide adaptive and personalized support to students.

A major part of the data is not structured. Data coming from student management systems or learning management systems comes from logs, in structured format where certain algorithms can be applied to mine the data. However, the data coming from student interactions with physical resources, conversation with peers, checking Facebook, going on Twitter, all that comes in different formats. To aggregate all those disparate data structures to make sense and identify relation to learning creates challenges for ubiquitous-learning-based adaptive and personalized learning environments. Most of this data is so unstructured and so large that processing it becomes extremely difficult. Various educational data mining approaches have emerged as solutions where patterns are identified that were not known before. Such patterns can be ad hoc, which means, they are recognised in real-time from the actions of a number of students. If many students have generated similar patterns, then the adaptivity and personalization mechanism checks whether those patterns are indicating some meaningful information.

The whole process of trying to identify the patterns is also quite complex. Once such patterns are identified by the mechanism, a great deal of training may be required on the part of the teachers to understand it before they can decide what kind of support the students need. In ubiquitous learning environments, where students may be learning in different places, it becomes important to provide support for time-sensitive learning process. As students move from one learning activity or assessment task to another in the ubiquitous environment, they can encounter a range of difficulties. However, it is likely that they may not ask for any help, since access to a teacher in real time could be seen as difficult to achieve. So if a teacher wants to proactively assist the students when they are not asking for help, they need access to all relevant data, both real time data and the historical learning information to be able to understand the context in which a particular student is experiencing the problem. The adaptivity and personalization mechanism needs to provide the analysis of such data in real time. This is where the context of learning analytics in ubiquitous environments plays significant role.

Test your understanding

- What are the basic differences between mobile learning and ubiquitous learning?
- Provide one learning scenario inside classroom that would qualify as ubiquitous learning.

Reflection

- Which of these scenarios will justify ubiquitous learning better; watching a video of car repair on a cellphone while enjoying the breeze of fresh air in the backyard of your home, or watching that same video in a car garage with the car standing there with open hood? Please justify your answer.
- Can social media play any important role in learning? If yes, how? If not, why not?

Learning analytics in ubiquitous environments

Learning analytics in ubiquitous environments, or "ubiquitous learning analytics" discovers, analyses and makes sense of different types of data about the student, what instruction they are currently receiving and in what kind of environment they are currently learning. The data is received from multiple sources, both from computer systems and from different types of sensors, and the ubiquitous learning analytics analyzes that data to identify evidence of learning.

Ubiquitous learning analytics discovers various types of information, such as past record and real time information about students' capabilities, preferences and competencies. Students' capabilities are different for different learning tasks. Students' preferences also change. This is natural for humans. For example, people do not like the same song all the time or eat the same food day after day. Similarly, study-related preferences also change and it is important for adaptivity and personalization mechanisms to use ubiquitous learning analytics to identify student preferences in ubiquitous learning environments. As students make progress in learning, they start to gain competence in that particular topic. Students' location is another factor the ubiquitous learning analytics analyses in order to identify what learning activities students have encountered at what location, where they are now, and then what next location would be the most appropriate for the next learning activity. The next factor analyzed is the technology students have at their disposal at the time of learning, such as a tablet or a mobile phone or a desktop computer. Another type of technology that is analyzed is what is available surrounding the learner, such as various sensors that can give information about the students' environment, about the noise level, visibility and so on, which can be helpful in determining what kind of learning activities would be suitable in that environment at that particular moment. One more factor discovered by ubiquitous learning analytics is the changes in the students' situational aspects. This includes identifying the actual environment in which an individual student is, such as a library, a museum, a classroom, a laboratory, or at home, whether a student is alone or in a group, whether a lecture going on or a discussion or whether the student is working without any other intervention, and so on. This enables the adaptivity and personalization mechanism to customize learning activities to suit that specific situation.

Additional information discovered by ubiquitous learning analytics that can help adaptivity and personalization mechanism includes a student's background skills, the type of learning that student has attempted, how much the student has learnt the concept, how much time was taken by the student to learn a particular concept and whether it was a reasonable time for that kind of learning? Did assessment conclude that the concept was really learnt? The evidence of learning activities can be used to see what kind of learning activities the student undertook. What kind of resources were used by the student? All these different items can enable the adaptivity and personalization mechanism to identify where the gaps are in the student's knowledge and skills, where he/she is having problems, where his or her actions are not matching with his/her abilities, capabilities and competencies.

After discovery, the next step in ubiquitous learning analytics is the analysis. The data received during the discovery step is analyzed student actions. What kind of interactions the student has with peers and instructors? What interactions the student has with physical objects, and in which learning activities are they being used? What online information the student is accessing on mobile device and in which learning activity is it being used? How the student's preferences changing, and whether some trends can be detected in those changing preferences? What are the changes in the student's skill and knowledge levels? The changes in the student's skill and knowledge levels can be analyzed in two ways: explicitly and implicitly. Explicit analysis includes data from assignments, quizzes, final exam and other similar formal procedures. Implicit analysis, on the other hand, attempts to find the changes in skill and knowledge levels through looking at evidence from micro-level activities, such as browsing Facebook, reading tweets on Twitter, having conversation on Skype, or other similar informal activities, and then using that information in subsequent learning activities.

Then comes the making sense of the analysis. The adaptivity and personalization mechanism needs to observe those patterns in the analysis that can give evidence for measurable learning. This is important because different students learning the same concept and doing the same learning activity would take different approaches to learning and would learn differently because of their different aptitudes, attitudes, and other characteristics. For example, to learn how sound travels across different materials, such as from solid to liquid, a student who has visual orientation, may want to see this in action in a video and explain the results. Another student with psychomotor orientation may want to try it with dipping a metal rod in an aquarium and bang it to see if fish react. A cognitively oriented student may want to consider the physics behind this phenomenon to understand it. Even further, a student with a medically minded attitude may want to see how sound travels from the bones of middle ear to the liquid in the inner ear.

Test your understanding

- Identify at least three different types of data sources that can be used in learning analytics when a student is exploring artifacts in a museum.
- What are three main steps od ubiquitous learning analytics?

Learning analytics in learning programming

Let us take another example of learning analytics, this time in learning a programming language, and see how learning analytics can improve the process of learning programming. Learning analytics can help in understanding how different students learn programming and what are effective ways of learning for different students.

First we shall look at why it is important to understand how different students learn programming, and how this understanding can help in helping individual students. Typically, in a classroom, when students complete a programming assignment, what teachers get is the final product. While it is possible for teachers to assess that completed assignment to identify whether the student knows the concepts and skills covered in that assignment or not, it is not possible for them to find out which particular areas of that assignment student had lots of problems, which parts the student was able to do quickly, which parts took lot of time, how the student made progress during completion of the assignment, which areas of the assignment the student is still not sure about even if he or she has completed it successfully, and so on. What it means is that the teachers are then not able to pinpoint exact weaknesses of the students and what particular support and feedback will be the most effective. This is because they have only looked at the final product and not the process by which that final product was completed.

Learning analytics enables the adaptivity and personalization mechanism of a learning environment for programming to observe the process of writing code by the student. It allows the identification of patterns that differentiate a novice programmer from an expert programmer, for example, the differences in the design of the UML diagram that the student creates at the start of the assignment and the changes he/she makes throughout the process of completing the assignment, the process of debugging the code, the types of testing the student does to validate the code, the documenting efforts, the code optimization efforts, and finally the self-regulation efforts which provides information about how the student managed the whole learning and assignment completion process. It also shows the pathway of entire learning process, compare it with the pathways of other students, look at the patterns of the best practices and accordingly make recommendations to the student for improvement.

Reflection

- Why is it important for adaptivity and personalization mechanism to understand the students' process of code writing instead of assessing only the final output?

Learning analytics for teachers

We have seen several examples of helping students through learning analytics. Let us now discuss how learning analytics can be used to support teachers in their task of teaching, particularly in ubiquitous environments where students and teachers may not be at the same location. We shall consider the role of a teacher in that situation and how we can make it effective for the teacher to provide pedagogical intervention in that kind of situation.

Ubiquitous learning environments allow students to learn at any time and any place, moving them toward more experiential learning such as learning by doing, interacting and sharing, and facilitating on-demand learning, hands-on or minds-on learning and authentic learning. These environments provide a huge amount of data about the students' learning processes as well as how students interact with their environment (see Kumar et al. 2015 for more details on big data learning analytics). This data can be used to help teachers better understand students' learning process and provide students with appropriate hints and assistance once they need them.

Adaptive and personalized learning environments can use this data to support teachers by providing them appropriate visualizations of students' characteristics and learning activities in real time and enable them to intervene as and when students need help. Technologies such as smart boards and smart tables are used to allow teachers to look at the students' data and interact with the students through natural interaction such as handwriting, touching, and gestures. Learning analytics is used to combine this interaction with the data received from external projectors, cameras and other similar technologies to enable teachers to use real-life objects for intervention in the students' learning process.

For example, the adaptivity and personalization mechanism of the ubiquitous learning environment can enable teachers to identify those students who are looking for help—students who have identified themselves by requesting help or those who are identified as requiring help by the mechanism. It can provide information about stalled students who started a learning activity but could not progress for some time, and those students who are deemed as "at risk" due to profile attributes such as low course prerequisites or low social interactions. In every case the mechanism provides the rationale for classifying the students in that category and provides teachers with recommendations for intervention. If the teacher does not agree with the recommendation and follows a different path of action, the mechanism learns from it for future recommendations.

Learning analytics also enables the adaptivity and personalization mechanism to provide overview of the students to the teachers at different levels. At the whole class level, the teacher is given a general sense of the whole class, in terms of prevalent learning styles, knowledge levels and progress, level of satisfaction, and other similar attributes that would help the teacher to understand the real-time status of learning process, and to get real time identification of when students start to fall behind or develop some certain needs that require pedagogical intervention. Teachers can also divide the students into various groups—predefined groups where students tend to be at similar stages in their coursework, or in the same learning activity, or with similar learning styles, and so on; and, dynamically created groups that are created based on specific queries from the teacher.

Smart learning environments

The next evolution of adaptive and personalized learning environments looks at how emerging technologies and paradigms such as learning analytics, ubiquitous technologies, cloud computing, cognitive profiling, immersive learning and others can help students achieve their full potential. While there is a clear demonstration that these advancements are helpful in improving learning, a far more fundamental change is needed in both the learning and the assessment processes to have a long-lasting effect. This is where smart learning environments have started to pervade the scene.

Smart learning environments go beyond simple application of technology. They provide an ecosystem of technology and pedagogy that involves active participation of teachers, parents and others into an individual student's learning process, provides continuous evidence of learning and gaining skills that are seamlessly transferred from one context to another, as individual students move from one learning context to another. Smart learning environments integrate evidence of learning happening in various shapes and forms to showcase competencies, such as in formal classrooms and laboratories; informal spaces, such as social media and small chit-chat during a hangout; workplace trainings that take place on demand; and any non-formal settings. They also focus on confidence in addition to competence, which is a key component of success. With increasing focus on 21st century skills, such as self-regulation, collaboration and critical thinking skills, smart learning environments integrate these skills with domain-based learning. The whole area of smart learning environments is in infancy but holds promise for the future of learning!

Learning activities

1. Select a topic in biology subject that may require students to observe activities outside of classroom.
2. Create a learning scenario where three students are learning that subject in three different locations.
3. Create a visualization for teacher, who is in his/her office, to show the progress of each student separately, comparatively, and in aggregate form.

Share your ideas with your colleagues and ask them to critique. Provide feedback to your colleagues on their ideas in return.

Links

International Association of Smart Learning Environments: www.iasle.net

References

Kumar, V. S.; Kinshuk; Somasundaram, T. S.; Boulanger, D.; Seanosky, J.; Vilela, M. F. (2015). Big Data Learning Analytics: A New Perspective. In Ubiquitous Learning Environments and Technologies, Heidelberg: Springer, 139–158.

Index

21st century skills 37, 175

A

ability of learn from analogies 48
ability to generate hypothesis 48
absence of the teacher 7
abstract concepts 21
abstract learning 23
academic performance 48
accessible 102, 140
Accessible Portable Item Protocol 144
action oriented tasks 22
action patterns 7, 126
action-driven 22
active learning 134
active observation 64, 66, 73
active participation 64, 106, 130, 175
Active RFIDs 106
activity pattern detector 55, 56
activity structures and frames 83
adaptive navigation guidance 10

Additive experimental design 156
ad-hoc study group 107
advance imitation 132
advance integration level 113
affective and psychomotor aspects 59
affective state 16, 162
analytical disciplines 133
analytical skills 37
animations 23, 34, 59, 62, 64, 67, 73, 74, 78, 84, 89, 96
annotations 83, 145
applied disciplines 34
applied inference engine 114
assessment process 31, 36, 166, 175
associative learning skill 10, 15, 38, 44, 50, 51, 52,
        56, 86, 87, 88, 98
asynchronous collaboration 119
audiogram 134
authentic learning 15, 146, 166, 173
authentic settings 146, 147
authoring tools 64, 144
automatic animations 73

automatic customization of learning 3
automatic modifications 12

B

Baddeley, Alan 44
barriers to education 3
Barwise, Jon 120
Behavioral attributes 10, 86
big data learning analytics 173
Bluetooth 106, 107
Brown, John Seely 63, 126

C

Caliper 144, 145
CanCore 141
case authoring 133, 136
case studies 15, 33, 50, 88, 140
central execution unit 44, 45
Certification 160
changing learning needs 167
check boxes 68
classroom based learning 133
cloud computing 175
coaching 63, 64, 127
cognitive abilities 9, 10, 43, 44, 52, 53, 54, 55, 56,
        64, 97, 98, 162
cognitive ability analyzer 55
cognitive ability detector 56
cognitive ability updater 56, 57
cognitive apprenticeship framework 63, 64, 72
cognitive attributes 10, 43, 86
cognitive load capacity 10, 89
cognitive models 63
cognitive overload 66, 71, 79, 80, 82
cognitive psychology 43
cognitive skills 26, 72, 73, 111, 125, 126, 127, 129,
        130, 132, 133, 134
cognitive trait model 53, 54, 55, 57
collaborative problem solving 119
Collins, Allan 63, 126
commercial implementations 153
Common Cartridge 144
comparative analysis 71
Comparison studies 161
competence levels 4, 53, 107
competence model 53
complementary resources 19
components of domain competence 22, 26, 125

composable ontology models 101
computer-based learning environments 21, 23, 30,
        59, 61, 68, 94, 96
conceptual level adaptation 60
connectivity dimension 96, 98, 99
constituents of domain competence 22
constructivist learning 77, 134
content; constraints 102; dimension 96, 107;
        experts 37; management systems (CMS) 4;
        manipulator 75; packages 141, 146, 147;
        renderer 75; repository 26; validator 74, 75
Content Packaging 141, 142, 145
content packaging format 142
content-based instruction 83
context-aware 101
contextual observation 132
contextual transfer 68
contextual understanding 25
control group designs 158
control-slave system 45
Cooper, Robin 120
co-operation 64
coordination dimension 96, 100
Cowen, Nelson 86
criterion-based evaluation 159
critical thinking 37; skills 175
crowdsourcing 105

D

data and privacy protection issues 11
data mining 55, 168
decision making skills 22, 63, 73, 126
deeper learning 132
deeper reflection 23
definitions 69
degree of evaluation 155
delayed feedback 64
designers' perspective 11
device; constraints 102; dimension 96, 98, 101
diagnosis and treatment of diseases 89
diagnostic accuracy 157
direct succession 69
discourse management 30, 32
discussion forums 4
divergent associative learning skills 51, 52, 56
domain; characteristics 86; competence 22, 24, 26,
        63, 66, 117, 121, 125, 131
Dublin Core Metadata Initiative 141

E

editable user model 13
EdNa 141
educational; framework 61, 62, 63, 72; games 62
effectiveness 5, 13, 44, 154, 158, 162, 163
efficiency 5, 13, 48, 49, 154, 158, 162
Elsom-Cook, Marc 130
embedding information 89, 90
environmental; context 24, 31, 32, 114; factors 24, 96, 113, 114
evaluation methods 153, 154, 155, 156, 158, 163
evaluation principles 154
events and episodes 120
evidence of learning activities 171
evidence of performance 16
excursions 69, 90
existence proofs 160
experimental research 157
expert inspection 158
explicit analysis 171
exploration; activities 77, 80; based learning 77, 78, 79, 81, 82, 83, 86, 88, 89; space 78, 79, 80, 81, 84, 87, 88; techniques 80;
exploratory evaluation 162
Extensible Markup Language (XML) 142
external evaluation 155, 157, 158, 159, 160, 161, 163

F

face-to-face; environment 19; teaching 4, 19
fading 63, 64, 127, 128
feedback/instruction quality 157
field dependency 46
flowchart 64, 73
fluid intelligence 45
formal assessment 19, 70
formal learning 19, 20, 33, 133
formation of higher order rules 45
future development 165

G

generic knowledge 64
gestures 121, 123, 174
GPS sensors 26
group learning 119
grouping techniques 83
guided discovery 130
guided instruction 130

H

Hannafin, Michael 6
hands-on skills 22
healthy ear 89
heart rate sensor 123
heart rate variability 10
holistic learning style 45
horizontal integration 113
human ear 89, 133, 134
human teachers 21, 23, 158, 160
human-computer interaction 32
Hypermedia based systems 26
hypothesis testing 156, 163

I

IEEE 141
IEEE Learning Object Metadata 141
image maps 34, 64, 68, 69, 79
immersive learning 175
implicit analysis 171
IMS; Content Packages 146, 147; Global Learning Consortium 142, 144; Learning Design 142, 146, 147; Learning Metric Profiles 145; Sensor API 145
individualized learning opportunities 167
inductive reasoning ability 10, 15, 44, 47, 48, 49, 50, 51, 52, 56, 86, 88, 98, 122
informal learning 20, 133
Informal learning activities 20
informal spaces 175
information processing speed 10, 15, 87, 121, 122
information space 79
Information tailoring techniques 83
innovation 130
Institution of Electrical and Electronics Engineers 141
instructional scaffolding techniques 83
instructional systems 26
integration of multimedia objects 65, 70, 71, 74
intelligent; assistance 133, 134; feedback 32; guidance 26; interactive simulations 134; tutoring systems 32, 112; objects 68, 69
interactional context 31, 32
interactive objects 68, 69
interactive videos 64
interface; design guidelines 63; representation 12
internal evaluation 155, 156, 157, 158, 159
internal frame of reference 46

International Organization for Standardization 141
Internet connectivity 94, 100
interoperable 140
interpretation of real life problems 132
interrelated conceptual atoms 113
intrinsic goal 20
introductory application level 113

J
just in time 21, 102

K
know-about 24, 25
know-how 22, 23, 24, 25, 26, 86
know-how-not 23
knowledge; hierarchy 69; representation 30, 32; structuring 32
know-when 24, 25, 26
know-where 24, 25, 26
know-why 22, 23, 24, 25, 86
know-why-not 23

L
lag; sequential analysis 157; sequential probability 157
learn by mistakes 23
learner constraints 102
Learning Analytics 143, 144, 169, 170, 171, 172, 173, 174; specifications 143
learning; anytime and anywhere 166; by analogy 49; by exploration 77, 78, 79; management systems 4, 26, 168; object repositories 140, 141; objects 88, 102, 104, 140, 141, 142; on demand 21, 133; outcomes 5, 45, 46, 51, 59, 88; sequence 4; styles 9, 12, 15, 16, 33, 38, 45, 46, 53, 97, 104, 143, 162, 174; theories 62; unit 4, 5, 69, 70, 99, 140
learning environment's behaviour 12
Learning Information Services 145
Learning Technology Standards Committee 141
Learning Tools Interoperability 144
level of agreement 158, 160
level of granularity 10
levels of adaptivity and personalization 13
life-long learners 20, 21
life-long learning 19, 20, 21, 111, 114
Lin, Taiyu 47

Littman, David 155
local expert model 114
local teacher 33, 37, 38
location constraints 102
lost in hyperspace 79
low working memory capacity 9, 46, 47, 52, 57, 87

M
measurable learning 171
measures of learning activities 144
media repository 167
memorisation of learned concepts 44
mental; abilities 9, 15, 48, 98; efforts 45, 79; map 113; operations 44
metadata 140, 141, 147, 148; repository 140; schema specifications 141; schemas 141
meta-learning skills 37, 79, 80
metaphors 25, 35, 49, 51
meta-tags 140
micro-level activities 171
Miller, George 86
misunderstandings 35, 120, 121, 122, 123, 124
mixed-initiative systems 114
mobile and ubiquitous learning 93
Mobile Authentic Authoring in IMS 147
modelling 63, 64, 126, 127
motivation 20, 21, 22, 38, 44, 77
multimedia capabilities 25
multimedia interface world 62
multiplatform; adaptation framework 101; environment 95, 96, 101

N
narrative problems 132
narrative questions 114
natural language; interaction 25; processing 23, 29
navigation techniques 80, 83
Newman, Susan E. 63
non-formal activities 19
non-verbal cues 23

O
objectival context 31, 36
observation and qualitative classification of phenomena 160
observational learning 105

online learning 3, 4, 33
online learning environment 7, 15, 36, 77
open and distance learning 133
open-ended arguments 25
open-ended scenarios 114
operational mistakes 114
opportunistic learning 103, 146
organizational policies 24
OSPAN 46
otoscope 134
outside assessment 160
oxygen level sensor 123

P

page level adaptation 60
paradigm shift 166
passive observation 64, 72
pattern matching 48, 49
Peck, Kyle 6
pedagogical goal 62
pedagogy shifts 166
performance; attributes 10, 86; metrics 159;
        model 53, 55
personality attributes 37, 38
personalized feedback 32
phonological loop 45
physical parameters 10, 98
physical skills 63, 125, 126
physical state 10
physical world 15
physiological attributes 10, 86
Piaget, Jean 77
pictorial virtual reality 64
pilot testing 159
plan recognition 32
pop-up windows 69
practical examples 84
pre-fetch 99
problem focused 21
problem solving 37, 48, 64, 89, 107, 116, 117,
        118, 119, 133, 135
problem space 114
procedural scaffolding techniques 83
process of elimination 49
product evaluation 158, 163
proof of correctness 156
pupil dilation 10, 53, 98
push buttons 68

Q

QR codes 106
quantitative methods 159
quasi-experimental designs 158
Question & Test Interoperability 144

R

radio buttons 68
rate of perspiration 10
RDF Triple 145
real-life objects 15, 174
real world situations 114
real-life scenarios 64
real-time context 4
reasoning 23, 24, 29, 32, 48
reasoning based learning 25
remedial content 8, 99
remote collaboration 111, 119, 120, 121, 122,
        123, 124
remote expert model 114
repetitive; learning 134; training 115, 117, 132
research issues 165
reusability 139, 143, 146

S

satisfaction 5, 174
scaffolding 81, 90, 118
scaffolding techniques 83
SCORM 142
selection of multimedia objects; for representing
        content 65, 66; to facilitate navigation
        65, 67
self-learning 70, 133
self-mediating 14
self-modifying 14
self-regulating 14
self-regulation 173, 175
sensitivity analysis 157
sensory channels 67
sensory motor skills 125
sentiment analysis 24
sequence of actions 7
sequence of operations 24
sequences of situations 120
sequencing of learning objects 142
serialistic learning style 46
Sharable Content Object Reference Model 142
shareable ontology 102

short-term memory 45, 46, 82

simple imitation 132

simulated real-world application level 113

simulation based learning 133

simulations 23, 34, 62, 64, 73, 78, 79, 83, 84, 89, 125, 134, 140

single group designs 158

situation theory 120

situational aspects 170

situations described through language 120

skills acquisition effectiveness 44

skin temperature 10, 98, 122, 123

smart; boards 173; learning environments 174, 175; tables 173

social environment 35

social media 20, 175

social monitoring 11

social platforms 4

societal norms 35

Soloway, Elliot 155

speed of learning 44

stimulating imagination 65

structured tasks and quantitative classification of phenomena 160, 163

student; characteristics 10, 74, 75, 86, 90, 107; management systems 143, 168; model 53, 54, 74, 85; profile 85, 122

student-computer interaction 30

student's actions 8, 11, 26; background 15, 170; competency 10; errors 7; location 16, 26, 101, 105; needs 8, 9, 16, 32, 66, 123; stress levels 10

symbolic representations 111, 112

synchronous remote collaboration 111, 119, 120, 121, 122, 123, 124

system; based adaptivity 13; functionality 153; initiated adaptivity 6; operations 7

systematic thinking 49

T

Tan, Qing 101

task oriented disciplines 63, 77

task solving patterns 63

teacher model 38

teacher-driven 4

teaching; approaches 4; process 31, 36; style 37, 38

teamwork 64

technological affordances 34

textual links 64

theoretical concepts 84

theory of constructivism 77

time constraints 102

time-sensitive learning 169

tools of the trade 64

transferability of learning 48

tutoring strategies 30, 61, 62

two-fold knowledge base 114

tympanic membrane 134

tympanogram 134

U

ubiquitous; environments 146, 166, 169, 173; learning analytics 169, 170, 171; learning environments 93, 146, 170, 173

user controlled animations 73

user initiated adaptability 6

user initiated animations 73

user model 13, 25, 97, 98

user model dimension 96, 97

user preference profile 95

V

verbal scaffolding techniques 83

vertical integration 113

videos 7, 16, 23, 35, 62, 64, 70, 71, 73, 95, 96, 132, 168

virtual reality 23, 62, 64, 66, 71, 73, 74, 90

visual content 34, 66, 67

visualization 22, 25, 26, 134, 143, 173

visual-spatial sketch-pad 45

W

wearable sensors 122

web-based learning 165

Web-OSPAN 46

Wizard of Oz 159

working memory; capacity 9, 10, 15, 38, 44, 45, 46, 47, 48, 49, 52, 53, 56, 57, 86, 87, 98, 122; storage system 45

world knowledge 128, 129

World Wide Web Consortium 145

Z

Zhang, Yuejun 141